ARMS AND ARMOUR OF THE ELIZABETHAN COURT

Thom Richardson

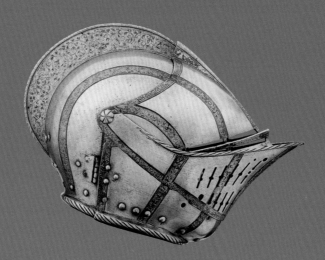

CONTENTS

Front cover: Burgonet of
the Smythe armour. II.84

Page 1: Armet of the
Hatton armour. II.77

Back cover: The
'Forget-me-not' gun,
wheellock pistol. XII.1764

FOREWORD

The Elizabethan court was a vibrant and colourful place, where the inherited traditions and technological skill that had characterised the Middle Ages came face to face with the decorative techniques of the Renaissance. This book is intended to show how the arms and armour in the collections of the Royal Armouries can be studied to gain an insight into this creative and dynamic period. It is not a complete catalogue of everything that survives, as that would make a much larger publication, but it draws on some of the most important pieces in the national collection. To some extent the picture that these objects present is skewed by the history of the collections: they have been acquired over a very long period of time. Originally chance played a large part in determining which objects survived, but later, when the role of the museum was beginning to be understood, the interests and intentions of successive curators have shaped the content of the collections.

The Royal Armouries' collection is founded on the historical armoury at the Tower of London, which by the end of the 14th century had become the national arsenal. The armoury was a working one, in a constant state of flux with new material coming in, arms being issued, and older material being discarded. A major change took place early in the 16th century, in parallel with the modernisation of the English army under Henry VIII, and little of the earlier armoury survives. The core of the armoury is preserved from that time, so the munition arms and armour of the later 16th century are available for study in profusion. Much of the arms and especially armour of the court gravitated to the royal palaces after the death of their original owners, and a very substantial proportion of this material was moved to the Tower during the Civil Wars of the 17th century. Because the individual owners of so many pieces can be identified, I have chosen to organise it by its owners, and briefly describe their roles within the court, government and army of the day.

The aim has been to maximise the amount of images while minimising the number of words, and a substantial but not exhaustive amount of graphic material from other collections has been included, since I believe that the objects held by the Royal Armouries, and indeed all museums, must be viewed in their context, and contemporary illustrative material is held in many different museums across the world. I have used the technical vocabulary of arms and armour throughout, but provided a glossary of the terminology at the end of the book.

Thom Richardson
Deputy Master, Royal Armouries

INTRODUCTION

The period from the death of King Henry VIII in 1547 to the accession of King James I in 1603 was one of great opulence in England. The wealth and the ostentatious display that went with it was reflected in the arms and armour of the period. It was the end of the great age of plate armour, in which the technology of steel manufacture reached its apogee, and the decoration of armour surfaces with etching and gilding was at its most lavish. The resurgence of Classical art which had begun in 14th century Italy provided a rich classical heritage on which the art of the age was founded. England was ruled by the surviving children of Henry VIII, briefly and nominally by his only surviving son, Edward VI (reigned 1547–53), then his two surviving daughters, Mary (reigned 1553–58) and Elizabeth (reigned 1558–1603). Neither of the women had armour made for them, but they presided over a thriving court in which the wearing of armour and arms not only reflected the fashionable tastes of the nobility, but also their military careers. Many of the politicians and courtiers were warriors too, and the age was one of almost continual conflict as the wars of religion between Catholics and Protestants were played out on the European stage.

The reign of Henry VIII had changed the character of arms and armour in England in many ways: the English army was transformed from an essentially medieval one, armed with longbow and bill, to a modern one armed with pike and harquebus. The development of firearms tactics and technology, especially the widespread introduction of the wheellock mechanism, had revolutionised warfare, making the use of pistols and calivers on horseback commonplace, while infantry pikemen were supplemented by 'shot' armed with matchlock firearms. Armourers followed these trends, and new, simple munition-quality armour for the battlefield came into use. The quality of armour in England was also transformed by Henry's establishment of a royal workshop, the Almain Armoury at Greenwich, staffed by continental armourers recruited from the major European centres, who made armour of the highest quality both of materials, manufacture and decoration for the king and his court.

◄ Portrait of Henry VIII after Holbein

Oil on panel, English, late 16th century. I.51

EDWARD VI AND THE TUDOR SUCCESSION

The later years of the reign of Henry VIII were dominated by his quest for a male heir. Yet for all his efforts, which encompassed divorce, six marriages and the establishment of the Church of England, the Tudor male line lasted only six years after his death.

EDWARD VI (1537–53)

Son of Henry VIII and his third wife, Jane Seymour, Edward VI reigned briefly from 1547–53. As he acceded to the throne at the age of nine, his reign was under the regencies first of Edward Seymour, Duke of Somerset, then from 1550 John Dudley, Earl of Warwick and Duke of Northumberland. On his death, following the nine-day rule of Lady Jane Grey, daughter of the Duke of Suffolk and wife of Dudley's son Guilford, he was succeeded by his Catholic half-sister Mary, daughter of Henry VIII and Katherine of Aragon.

Edward's reign included war with Scotland, which started with the defeat of the Scots at Pinkie in 1547, but ended with alliance between France and Scotland and withdrawal of English forces from Scotland and the loss of Boulogne in 1550.

◀ Portrait of King Edward VI, aged 9, unknown artist, about 1547.

© National Portrait Gallery, London

▶ Lower lames of a tasset

For a youth, possibly for Edward VI. English, Greenwich, about 1550. Purchased from the Pembroke armoury at Wilton House, 1951. III.1267

Edward VI had at least one armour made at Greenwich. This one is a miniature version of the light cavalry armours that were popular for adults in the middle of the 16th century. The helmet and gauntlets are missing. Its cuirass is made with articulated plates in the form called an 'anime', which probably reflects the interest in the arms and armour of ancient Rome and is intended to look like the ancient armour we now call the *lorica segmentata*. These animes were popular from about 1540–60. The borders are gilt, and the lower plates of the tassets are embossed and gilded with chevrons.

A fragment of another armour, the lowest two plates of the right knee, shows that at least one other small field armour was made at Greenwich during the short reign of Edward VI, and that it was decorated in exactly the same way as the other one. It is most likely that this is all that remains of an armour of Edward VI; Pembroke, as the young king's guardian, was highly influential and acquired one of Henry VIII's last armours for the armoury at Wilton.

◀ Three-quarter anime armour

For a boy of about twelve years old, possibly Edward VI. English, Greenwich, about 1550. Purchased 1957 from the collection of the Earls of Mount Edgecumbe at Cothele House, Cornwall. II.178

▶ Page from the Jacob Album showing the field armour of the Earl of Rutland with its anime cuirass, one of the two armours in the Album captioned MR, showing the images were made during Queen Mary's reign.

© Victoria and Albert Museum, London

WILLIAM HERBERT, 1ST EARL OF PEMBROKE (1506/7–70)

▲ Portrait of young William Herbert in a Greenwich armour.
National Museum Wales

Pembroke was a Tudor courtier, entered service with Charles Somerset 1st Earl of Worcester and became one of Henry VIII's Gentlemen Pensioners by 1526. He married Anne Parr, sister of Catherine, Henry VIII's sixth and last wife, in about 1537, and was knighted in 1544. In the same year he acquired Wilton House in Somerset and began building there, and served at the siege of Boulogne. He served as MP for Wiltshire from 1547, and was guardian to the young Edward VI, by whom he was created Knight of the Garter in 1549 and Earl of Pembroke in 1551. He avoided supporting Lady Jane Grey and won Queen Mary's favour by putting down Thomas Wyatt's rebellion of 1554. In 1557 he led an English army to France, assisted the Spanish capture of St Quentin, and bore Queen Elizabeth's sword on her entry into London in 1558. As well as acquiring lands in South Wales he profited from risky merchant adventures, investing in Sir Hugh Willoughby's expedition to find the Northeast Passage in 1552, and John Hawkins slaving expedition to Africa in 1563. He may have founded the carpet-weaving factory at Wilton, staffing it with fugitive Flemish weavers.

His most magnificent Greenwich armour, which includes the only full horse armour made at Greenwich, has an anime cuirass with a solid plackart, and is now in Glasgow Museums and Art Galleries at Kelvingrove, no. 1939.65.a–d. It is not recorded in the Jacob Album, and almost certainly pre-dates the Album. Yet another anime cuirass made for the Earl at Greenwich survives in the Royal Ontario Museum, Toronto.

Pembroke's light field armour is identified in the Wilton inventory of 1558 as 'a black anymate parcell gilte with the vambraces splinted in partes without gauntletts'. The semi-anime cuirass has a very complex internal structure including hinges, sliding rivets, leathers and springs by which all the plates of the cuirass are made extra flexible. Similar constructions are found in armours made by members of the Negroli family of Milan for King Charles I of Spain

◄ Half armour of
William Herbert

North Italian modified in
England, about 1555.
Purchased 1981, from the
Reaymaekers collection,
Belgium, formerly from
the armoury of the Earls
of Pembroke at Wilton
House. II.358, associated
mail sleeves III.1427–8

► Rear view of the
armour. Most unusually
the gorget is fitted over
the cuirass, fastened in
place with pierced studs
and pins.

▲ Detail of the internal articulation, showing the extent of the modifications, probably done at Greenwich, to make this complex mechanism work.

▶ Internal view, showing the complex articulation of the breastplate.

and Henri II of France. The complex construction evidently did not work perfectly as it shows signs of having been altered, possibly at the royal workshop at Greenwich. It is likely that the vambraces were added at Greenwich too, and they are also of an unusual, splinted design. The modification of the armour at Greenwich recalls Henry VIII's last Italian armour, which was also modified at Greenwich to fit the king, and was also preserved at Wilton House. Pembroke also had a light field armour, an unusual type for Greenwich at this time, as it had a solid breastplate rather than the splinted 'anime' found on other contemporary field armours. It is either 'my lords felde armor of Erasmus makeing parcel gilte with the furniture' or 'an armor for my lord Herbert enamelled and parcel gilte with his furniture' in the Wilton House inventory of 1558. The close helmet has a most unusual barred visor with a pivoted upper bevor like the upper lame of a falling buffe not found on any other Greenwich helmet.

Pembroke's son Henry Herbert (1538–1601), 2nd Earl of Pembroke, accompanied his father to St Quentin in 1557, and succeeded to the earldom in 1570. He was appointed Lord Lieutenant of Wiltshire and Lord President of the Council of the Marches of Wales in 1586. His Greenwich armour, which was preserved along with the rest of the family armoury at Wilton House until the early 20th century, is now in the Metropolitan Museum of Art, New York, no. 32.130.5. It appears in the Jacob Album after Sir Christopher Hatton's first armour (which is dated 1585), but appears to have been executed a few years before that, about 1580. It is decorated with broad etched and gilded bands, with a sinuous pattern of serpents on the bright ground between the bands, and had on its shaffron an escutcheon of the complete arms of the Earls of Pembroke.

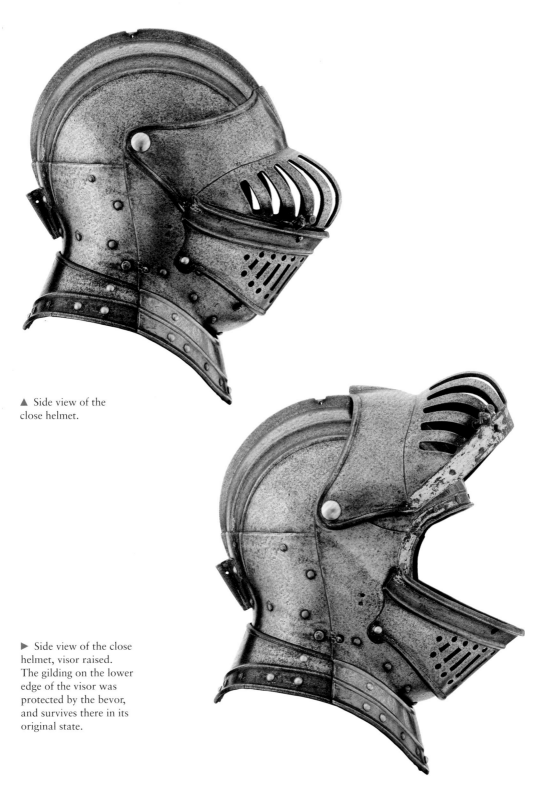

▲ Side view of the close helmet.

▶ Side view of the close helmet, visor raised. The gilding on the lower edge of the visor was protected by the bevor, and survives there in its original state.

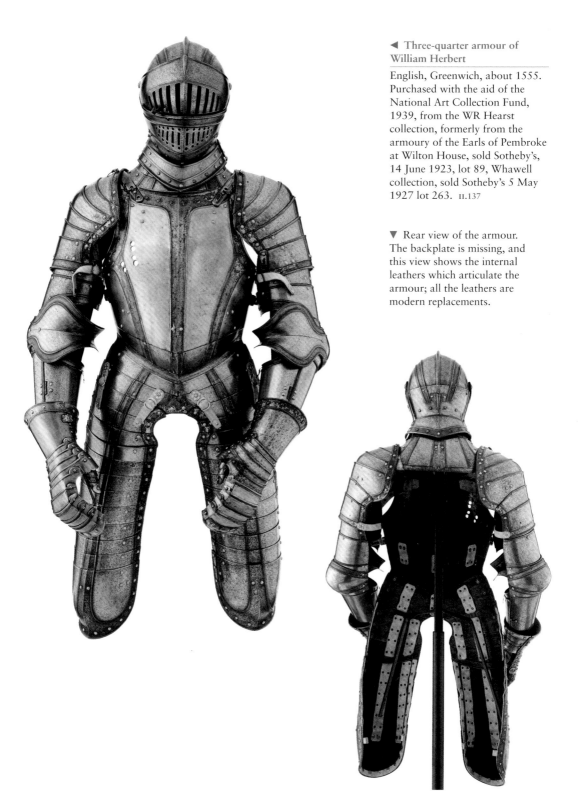

◄ Three-quarter armour of William Herbert

English, Greenwich, about 1555. Purchased with the aid of the National Art Collection Fund, 1939, from the WR Hearst collection, formerly from the armoury of the Earls of Pembroke at Wilton House, sold Sotheby's, 14 June 1923, lot 89, Whawell collection, sold Sotheby's 5 May 1927 lot 263. II.137

▼ Rear view of the armour. The backplate is missing, and this view shows the internal leathers which articulate the armour; all the leathers are modern replacements.

WILLIAM SOMERSET, 3RD EARL OF WORCESTER (1526–89)

Worcester was in early life principal esquire to King Henry VIII, and later attended the coronations of Edward VI, Queen Mary and Elizabeth I. He fought with his father the 2nd Earl in France in 1544 and 1546, carrying Henry VIII's helmet and lance at Calais. He was knighted by Edward VI at his coronation, and married Christian, daughter of Lord North in 1549. He was a supporter of Lady Jane Grey as well as Queen Mary in 1553, and served in the army in France under the Earl of Pembroke in 1557. He attended parliament, but as a Catholic he was given no offices under Elizabeth, though he was created a Knight of the Garter in 1570. In 1573 he attended the christening of the daughter of Charles IX in Paris on Queen Elizabeth's behalf, and in 1586 was one of the commissioners at Fotheringay for the trial of Mary Queen of Scots. As late as 1588 he was still raising cavalry, six lances and 26 light horse, for the English army. His residence was Raglan Castle in Wales, which he substantially modernised.

▲ Portrait of William Somerset, 3rd Earl of Worcester in his Greenwich armour, 1569.

Private collection/Bridgeman Images

Worcester's armour is a remarkable field garniture made in the royal workshop at Greenwich under John Kelte the Master Workman there from 1567–76. If all its heaviest elements are assembled together it is the heaviest known armour in the world at 59.1 kg (130 lb 4 oz), and even assembled as a conventional field armour it is unusually heavy at 38.6 kg (85 lb 1 oz), some 20% above the weight of a standard armour. The armour comprises a complete field armour with a series of extra pieces, a wrapper for the armet of the field armour, a set of saddle steels and half shaffron for his horse, and burgonet and buffe for light cavalry use on the battlefield, and an alternative heavy gorget and cuirass together with a burgonet and buffe for wear either on the battlefield or perhaps intended for siege use. The portraits show that the armour was originally purple with recessed bands of gilt scallops. It appears in the Jacob Album in the Victoria and Albert Museum, London, and the page of extra pieces

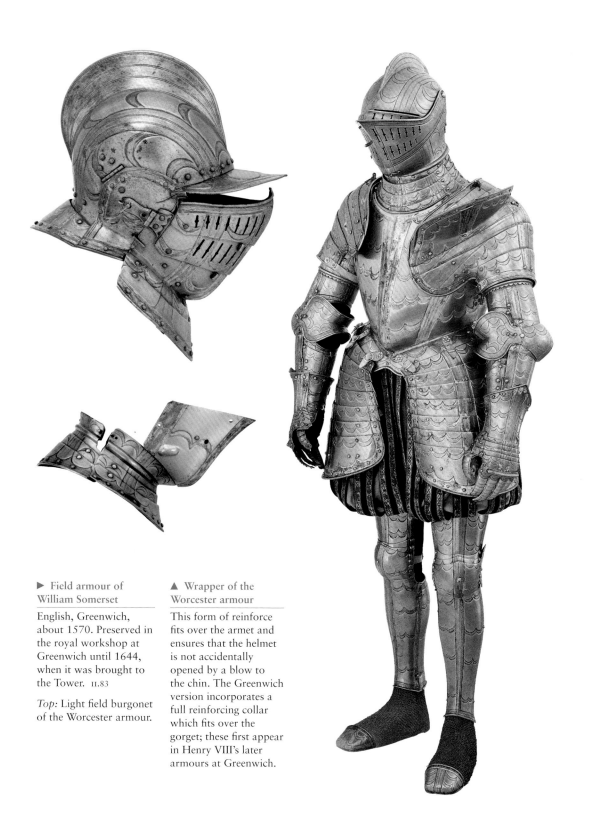

▶ Field armour of William Somerset

English, Greenwich, about 1570. Preserved in the royal workshop at Greenwich until 1644, when it was brought to the Tower. II.83

Top: Light field burgonet of the Worcester armour.

▲ Wrapper of the Worcester armour

This form of reinforce fits over the armet and ensures that the helmet is not accidentally opened by a blow to the chin. The Greenwich version incorporates a full reinforcing collar which fits over the gorget; these first appear in Henry VIII's later armours at Greenwich.

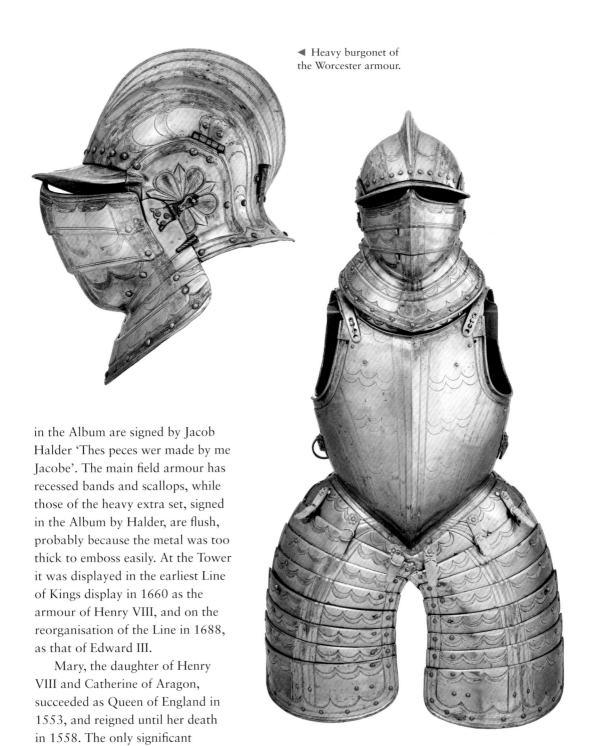

◀ Heavy burgonet of the Worcester armour.

in the Album are signed by Jacob Halder 'Thes peces wer made by me Jacobe'. The main field armour has recessed bands and scallops, while those of the heavy extra set, signed in the Album by Halder, are flush, probably because the metal was too thick to emboss easily. At the Tower it was displayed in the earliest Line of Kings display in 1660 as the armour of Henry VIII, and on the reorganisation of the Line in 1688, as that of Edward III.

Mary, the daughter of Henry VIII and Catherine of Aragon, succeeded as Queen of England in 1553, and reigned until her death in 1558. The only significant military activity of her reign was the loss of Calais to the French in 1558.

▲ Heavy field armour of the Worcester armour.

▲ Plackart of the Worcester armour,
for the field and tourney.

▼ Two pages from the Jacob Album showing
the Worcester armour and its extra pieces.
Image from *An Almain Armourer's Album*.
London 1905. © Royal Armouries

▶ Shaffron

Half shaffron of the
Worcester armour. VI.50

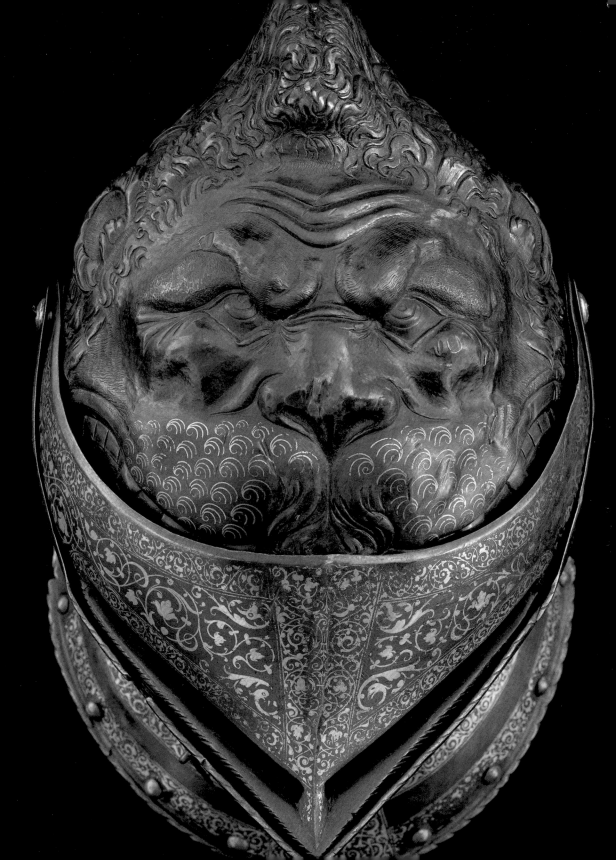

THE EUROPEAN MONARCHIES

HENRI II OF FRANCE (1519–59)

Unlike Henry VIII, the French King François I of France had a son and heir, Henri II, who succeeded him in 1547. His reign was marked by angry suppression of Protestants, wars with Charles V and Philip II of Spain (Queen Mary's future husband), and marriage of his son to Mary Queen of Scots in the hope of gaining a dynastic advantage in the potential English power vacuum. Despite this he was created a Knight of the Garter in England in 1551. A great lover of the tournament he died after a joust in 1559 when a shattered lance entered the sight of his visor and passed through his eye into his brain.

It is possible that the 'Lion Armour' was made for Henry II. The armour, damascened in gold, and decorated with embossed lions' heads, stands among the finest examples of embossed armour of the Renaissance. It was probably once a small garniture, with interchangeable pieces for the field and tournament; the helmet is marked with sword-cuts probably received in the tourney. One extra piece of the armour, a burgonet, is recorded in a drawing and in a still life which includes other pieces of armour from the French royal collection, and shows that the armour could have been mounted as a light field armour. The original foot

◀ Sword-cuts from use in the tourney appear on the top of the close helmet of the Lion Armour. II.89.

▼ Drawing of the lost burgonet of the Lion Armour, possibly French, 19th century. I.393

▼ *Below right:* Still life, attributed to the circle of Madeleine Boulogne (1648–1710), including the lost Lion Armour burgonet among other pieces of armour from the French royal collection.
Courtesy Christie's, London

defences are missing, and the toe-caps shown with the armour today came from the Royal Armoury in Madrid in the 19th century; they belong to an embossed and damascened Milanese armour of the 1580s that was presented to Philip III of Spain by the Duke of Savoy in 1606.

The Lion Armour is so unusual that scholars are unable to agree even on the country in which the armour was made. It has many features in common with Italian embossed armour makers of the mid-16th century, and could be by one or more members of the Negroli family though it is not clearly comparable with any of their signed work. Certainly more than one hand was involved in the embossed decoration: the panel at the top of the breastplate and backplate is of a much finer, sharper embossing than the decoration on the rest of the armour. Some authorities have suggested a French maker, possibly Benedict Clesze, while others have suggested Flanders as its origin, and it is comparable with the work of Eliseus Libaerts of Antwerp. It was made at about the time when the French royal family were transferring their patronage from the Negroli to Libaerts for fine armour commissions. How and when it reached England is unknown, but it appears in a number of 17th-century portraits, the earliest of which was painted in about 1620, the latest in 1669.

▼ Detail of the backplate.

The Lion Armour

Possibly of King Henri II of France, probably Italian, about 1550. Displayed from 1768 as the armour of Charles II in the Line of Kings display at the Tower. Formerly in the French royal collection, the English royal collection under King Charles I, and most probably the 'Rich Guilte Armor delivered to Generall Cromwell' by Edward Annesley in 1644. II.89

The toe-caps are also embossed and gilded with lion masks, but from a different armour. The pierced holes around the rear edge are for the attachment of a mail sabaton.

The armour is decorated overall with embossed lions. The gold inlay or 'Damascening' on the armour is also of the highest quality.

► Portrait of an unknown man wearing the Lion Armour, painted either by a Flemish artist working in England or by an English artist working in the Flemish style, about 1620.

The National Musuem of Art of Romania, Bucharest

► Portrait of Edward Montagu, 2nd Earl of Manchester, wearing the Lion Armour.

© Ashmolean Museum, University of Oxford

► Forlorn Hope medal of 1643

Showing the Lion Armour worn by both King Charles I and his son, Charles Prince of Wales, the future Charles II. XVIII.564

PHILIP II OF SPAIN (1527–98)

Spain was ruled by Charles V's son, Philip the Prudent, throughout the later Tudor period. Philip was also King of England following has marriage in 1554 to Queen Mary I, and the couple reigned together for her few remaining years. Philip's reign was a golden age of art and culture in Spain, which was at the time the wealthiest and most powerful kingdom in Europe. Philip organised a Mediterranean alliance with Venice, Savoy, the Papacy and the Knights of St John of Malta which fought a series of naval campaigns against the Turks culminating in victory at the battle of Lepanto in 1571. In the Low Countries he pursued a long war to suppress the revolt of the Seventeen Provinces of the Netherlands. In the Iberian Peninsula he conducted a swift campaign of conquest against Portugal, assuming its kingship after victory at the battle of Alcantara in 1580. After Queen Mary's death Philip lost his rights in England. Philip sent four armadas to attempt to conquer England, but all of them failed. Many of Philip's armours survive in the Real Armeria in Madrid. Despite his time as king, he never appears to have had an armour made at Greenwich.

▲ Philip II of Spain c. 1580.
© National Portrait Gallery, London

MAXIMILIAN II OF AUSTRIA (1527–76)

Threatened by Ottoman expansion in the east, Maximilian moved his capital to Vienna and raised armies to defend the Empire from the Turks. Relations with his cousin Philip of Spain were always difficult, though his daughter Anna became Philip's fourth wife in 1570, and he was unable or unwilling to intervene in support of the allies in the Lepanto campaign.

ELIZABETH'S COURT

Following the death of Henry VIII the salaried armourers at the royal workshop at Greenwich continued to work for the monarch. However Henry's heir, Elizabeth I, did not require armour for herself and she had neither husband nor son to provide for. The queen found a profitable way of running the workshop by selling expensive licences to her favoured courtiers permitting them to order armours from the royal workshops. The Royal Armouries has the finest collection of these Elizabethan courtiers' armours.

Elizabeth, daughter of Henry VIII and Anne Boleyn, succeeded as Queen of England in 1558, and reigned until her death in 1603. Her reign started with the brief occupation of Le Havre in 1562–3, after which England avoided military action until 1585 when an army was sent under her favourite, Robert Dudley, Earl of Leicester, to the Netherlands to aid the Protestant Dutch rebels again Philip II of Spain. This was combined with naval action against Spain in the Caribbean and a raid on Cadiz. The Spanish riposte was the Armada campaign of 1588, which was defeated at sea by a combination of superior English seamanship and gunnery, poor planning on the part of the Spanish and inclement weather. After the defeat of the Armada England again allied with France under the protestant sympathiser Henri IV, and sent a series of expedition to the Continent. The first was led by Lord Willoughby d'Eresby against the Spanish in the Low Countries in 1589. The second was led by John Norreys into Brittany in 1591. The third was led by Robert Devereux, Earl of Essex, in 1591–2 to aid Henri IV at the siege of Rouen. All three ended in failure. Uprising in Ireland against Protestant English rule led to the Nine Years War, 1594–1603. Essex was again sent to lead the English army there in 1599, but returned against the Queen's orders and was replaced by Charles Blount, Lord Mountjoy, who completed the defeat of the rebels.

◀ Queen Elizabeth I, by an unknown English artist, circa 1588.
© National Portrait Gallery, London

ROGER, 2ND BARON NORTH
(1531–1600)

Lord North was a courtier who was an early favourite of Princess Elizabeth, by whom he was created a Knight of the Bath at her coronation in 1559. He undertook with Thomas Radcliffe, Earl of Sussex, a mission to Vienna in 1568 to invest Maximilian II with the Order of the Garter, and to make a final attempt at negotiating the queen's marriage to the Archduke Charles. He may have been sent with Francis Walsingham to France in 1570 to secure better terms for the Huguenots, and in 1574 was sent to France to congratulate Henri III on his accession. Remaining a favourite of the queen's, he joined Leicester and Sidney in their campaign to the Low Countries to support the Dutch rebels against Philip II in 1585.

One armour in the Jacob Album closely resembles this surviving armour, made for Lord North, but that this armour might have been made for him has been argued strongly over the years. The armour is decorated with recessed gilded bands, and is constructed with

▶ Field armour

Page 29: With decorated and gilt bands. English, Greenwich, about 1560. Old Tower collection.
II.82

▼ Pages from the Jacob Album showing the armour and extra pieces of Lord North.
© Victoria and Albert Museum, London

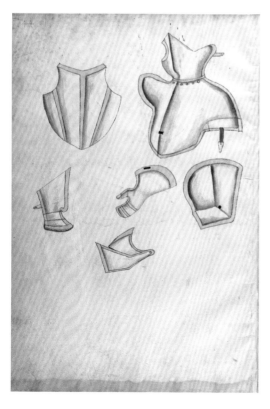

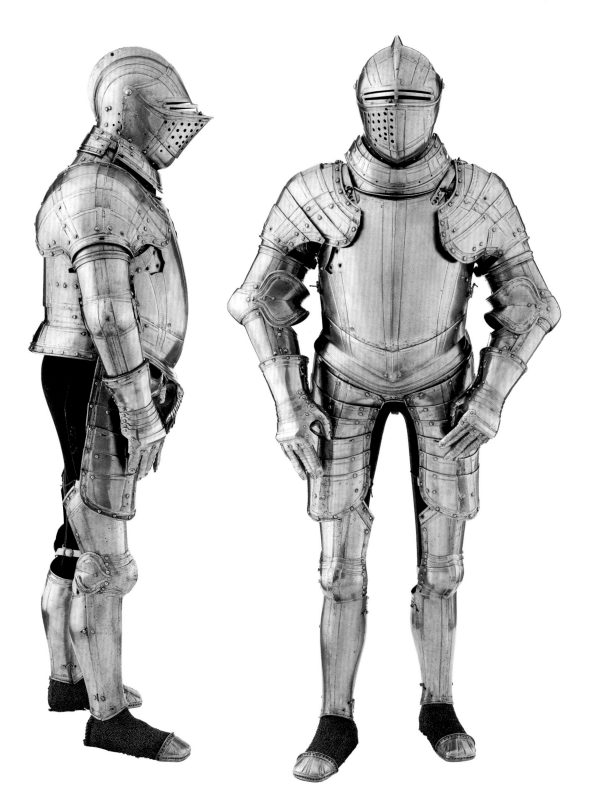

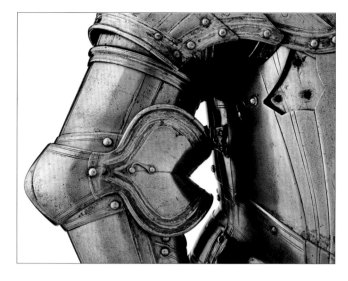

relatively long tassets and short cuisses (upper and lower thigh defences), suggesting a date of about 1560. There are a few detail differences: the borders are shown in the Album with roped edges, a fashion which came in about 1550, whereas the armour is made with the more conservative plain turned edges, and the knees and elbows are shown with embossed radial flutes, which the armour lacks. The armour was issued from the Tower in 1714 to the King's Champion at the coronation of King George I and again in 1727 to the champion at the coronation of George II. The office of King's Champion was held by successive members of the Dymoke family of Scrivelsby Court in Lincolnshire, Sir Lewis Dymoke (d. 1760) officiating at both of these coronations.

▲ The breastplate is reinforced by a plackart, fastened with studs and swivel hooks. This was designed to fit over the lance rest; though this is lost, the three holes in the breastplate to which it was attached by screws, and the cut-out in the plackart for it are clearly visible. The wing of the couter can also be detached using the studs and swivel hooks.

▶ Close helmet of the armour. The vacant rivet holes at the side of the bevor are for a lost visor prop, which engaged the nicks in the lower edge of the upper bevor, and for a sprung catch which fastened the bevor closed.

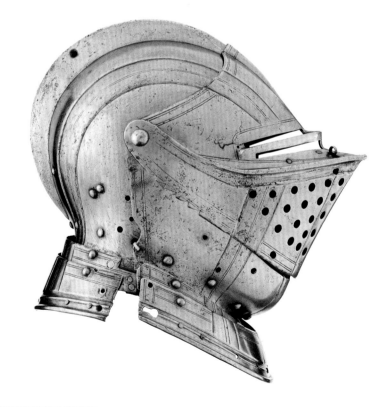

ROBERT RADCLIFFE, 5TH EARL OF SUSSEX (1573–1629)

Soldier and courtier, Sussex served under the Earl of Essex at Cadiz in 1596, as Earl Marshal in 1597, and was created Knight of the Garter in 1599 and made Colonel General of an army intended to counter a Spanish invasion that never materialised. Under James I he served as Lord Lieutenant of Essex.

His grandfather Robert, the 2nd Earl, commanded Edward VI's army against the Scots at the battle of Pinkie in 1547, while his uncle Thomas the 3rd Earl was Chief Governor of Ireland, and his father Henry, the 4th Earl, was Governor of Portsmouth.

▶ Portrait of Robert Radcliffe, 5th Earl of Sussex, called the 'White Knight', wearing a plain Greenwich armour, English, painted about 1593. 1.36

SIR CHRISTOPHER HATTON (1540–91)

Privy councillor, another favourite of Elizabeth, Hatton came to queen Elizabeth's attention when he performed in the Inner Temple in a play, *Gorbudoc*, in a cast which included Robert Dudley. In 1564 he became a Gentleman Pensioner, in 1571 MP for Higham Ferrers in Northamptonshire and by 1572 Captain of the Yeomen of the Guard. By 1578 he was a member of the Privy Council, and involved in the negotiations over the proposed marriage between Elizabeth and Henri Duke of Anjou, later King Henri III of France. Hatton was one of the party with Cecil (Baron Burghley), Leicester, Howard, Hunsdon and Walsingham sent to the Netherlands to negotiate the Treaty of Nonsuch, with the states general, in which England agreed to supply troops and money to the Dutch rebels.

▲ Miniature portrait of Sir Christopher Hatton by Nicholas Hilliard, about 1588–91.

© Victoria and Albert Museum, London

On the death of the Lord Chancellor Sir Thomas Bromley in 1587 the post was offered to the Earl of Rutland, owner of another Greenwich armour, but he died almost immediately. Hatton was next in line, and served as Lord Chancellor to Elizabeth from 1587–91. He was created a Knight of the Garter in 1588, and had three or four armours made at Greenwich. The first in the Album survives in the Royal Collection at Windsor castle, and is dated 1585. Hatton was given Ely Place in Holborn by the queen, and gave his name to the area of the City of London which is now known as Hatton Garden.

Hatton's first Greenwich armour survives in the Royal Collection at Windsor Castle, retains its original russet finish and is dated 1585. All that survives of the second of Sir Christopher Hatton's armours in the Jacob Album is the vamplate. It is decorated with broad etched and gilt bands of strapwork separated by true lovers' knots and Tudor roses, presumably an allusion to Hatton's love for his queen. His coat of arms is shown on the Album without the garter belt, showing the design was done before 1588.

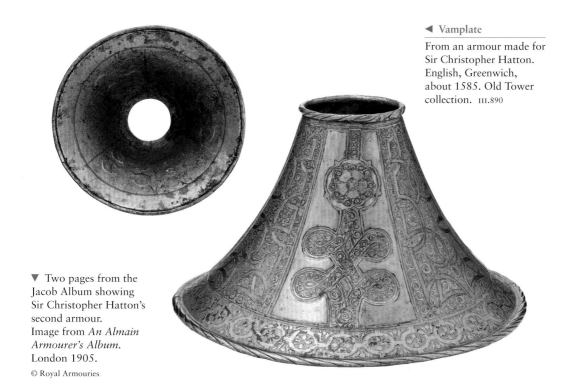

From an armour made for
Sir Christopher Hatton.
English, Greenwich,
about 1585. Old Tower
collection. III.890

▼ Two pages from the
Jacob Album showing
Sir Christopher Hatton's
second armour.
Image from *An Almain
Armourer's Album*.
London 1905.

© Royal Armouries

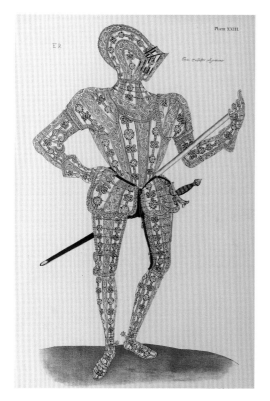

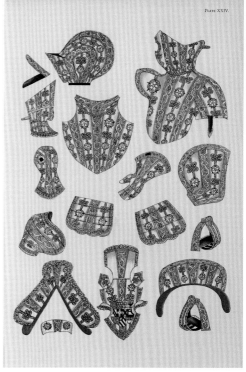

The third and fourth of Hatton's Greenwich armours are of identical form, one labelled 'Sir Christopher Hatton', the other 'My Lord Chauncelor', and therefore captioned in or after 1587 (or possibly designed for Sir Thomas Bromley before 1587). Both were field armours decorated with narrow etched and gilded bands, and provided with a plackart, burgonet and buffe, and a pair of long elbow gauntlets for wear over mail sleeves. The first has a pair of alternative long pauldrons, the second a pair of short extensions for the pauldrons attached by pierced studs and pins to the pauldrons of the main armour, and a set of saddle steels. Three more almost identical field armours are illustrated in the Jacob Album, and all were probably made in the years leading up to the Spanish Armada campaign of 1588. Presumably Hatton ordered two of these armours and gave one away. Of one of these armours only the armet, collar, arm defences and greaves survive, and they were incorporated in the armour of Sir John Smythe, which, as a light field armour, lacks those components. The combination of the two armours had occurred by at least 1714 when they were depicted together in a portrait of James Butler, 2nd Duke of Ormonde by Michael Dahl, now in the National Portrait Gallery. The armour was displayed as that of Henry IV in the Line of Kings at the Tower in the late 16th century.

▼ Two pages from the Jacob Album showing Sir Christopher Hatton's third armour.

© Victoria and Albert Museum, London

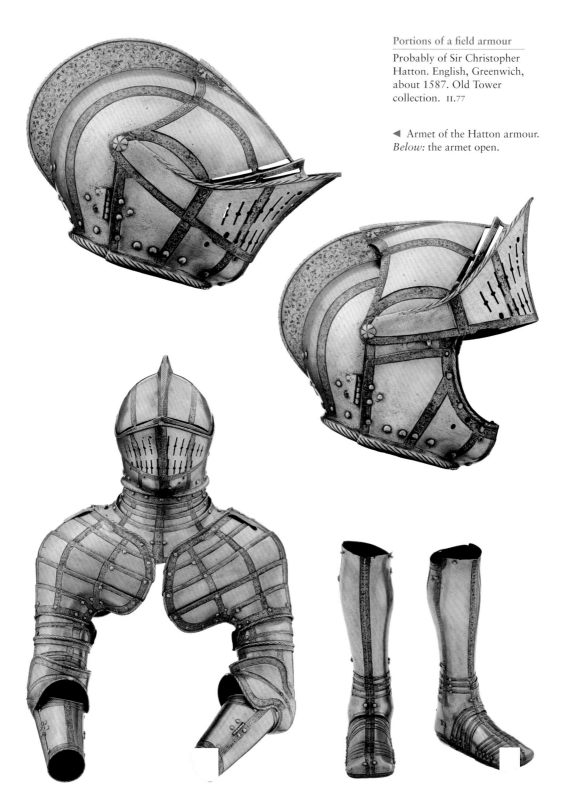

Portions of a field armour

Probably of Sir Christopher Hatton. English, Greenwich, about 1587. Old Tower collection. ɪɪ.77

◀ Armet of the Hatton armour. *Below*: the armet open.

Lee entered the service of Henry VIII as a clerk in 1545, was Clerk of the Armoury 1549–50, knighted in 1559, Master of the Armoury 1578–1611 and Master of the Ordnance in 1590, as well as acting as Queen Elizabeth I's personal champion 1559–90. He was created a Knight of the Garter in 1597. He had three armours made at the royal workshops at Greenwich, parts of two of which survive.

The first of Lee's Greenwich armours was a field garniture made 'beyond see', probably in Augsburg, provided with an armet and burgonet for cavalry use and a 'Spanish' morion and circular shield for infantry use, for which Halder made at Greenwich a set of extra pieces for the tourney, an armet with an alternative visor and a wrapper, grandguard, pasguard and manifer. None of this interesting armour survives, but it is closely related to the Smythe armour which likewise had Augsburg and Greenwich components.

▲ Portrait of Sir Henry Lee. Anglo-Flemish, late 16th century. I.379

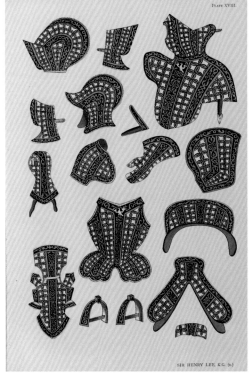

Lee's second Greenwich armour was a field armour with extra pieces for the tournament and field. It is captioned in Halder's hand 'Sr Henry Lee Mr of Tharmorie'. The surviving armet with its characteristic hinged cheekpieces is clearly the alternative tournament armet illustrated in the Album, with its narrow sight, brow reinforce and the pierced studs for attachment of the grandguard. It is decorated with bands of etched and gilt strapwork joined by linked quatrefoils. Other parts of the armour are in the Livrustkammaren, Stockholm, the burgonet and buffe, leg defences and half shaffron, while the locking gauntlet for the tourney is in the Hall of the Armourers and Brasiers Company of London, having been presented by a former Master of the Company in 1768. It is unknown how parts of the armour reached Sweden, but they were there by the mid-17th century, when they appear in a portrait of Count Neils Bielka (1624–84) in Skokloster Castle near Stockholm.

Lee's third armour is decorated like Hatton's with narrow bands of etched decoration, a running design of pines and pomegranates, with the letters AV for his mistress, Anne Vavasour, in several places. The armour survives almost complete in the collection of the Armourers and Brasiers Company. The design in the Jacob Album shows that these bands were originally intended to be enamelled in green and red, but no evidence of this finish survives.

◀ *Page 36:* Two pages from the Jacob Album showing Sir Henry Lee's second armour with its extra pieces. Image from *An Almain Armourer's Album.* London 1905.

© Royal Armouries

▶ Armet of
Sir Henry Lee

English, Greenwich, about 1580. Purchased from the Bernal collection, Christie's, 28 March 1855, lot 2701. IV.43

THE TOURNAMENT

The tournament was of fundamental importance to the early Tudor court. Early in his reign Henry VIII was an enthusiast, competing with the nobility of England and abroad for chivalric honour. To celebrate the birth of a son in 1511 a great tournament was held at Westminster in which the king, as 'Coeur Loyal' (loyal heart), achieved the best score in the jousts. Many of Henry's tournaments were linked with diplomacy, most extravagantly the 'Field of Cloth of Gold' of 1520 in which Henry and François I of France competed in the same team, and signed a peace treaty between the two nations. Other tournaments were held for entertainment, such as that staged in 1527 before the French ambassador and his delegation.

The events of the tournament in England in the 16th century were three: the joust, or tilt, the tourney and the foot combat over the barriers. The tilt, a barrier separating the contestants, had been introduced in the 15th century as a safety feature in the individual combat with lances on horseback that was the joust. Only one form of the joust was popular in England, called the Joust Royal or Joust of Peace (German *Gestech*). In Henry's reign it retained an archaic form of armour, including the great helm and a form of shield, neither of which forms of armour had been used by men-at-arms on the battlefield since about 1350.

A major change in armour style occurred in the 1520s in which both of these old-fashioned types of harness were discarded and replaced by a new set, based around the current form of field armour with the addition of extra pieces of 'pieces of exchange' which enabled a single armour to be configured for any of the events of the tournament and often for the battlefield as well. Throughout the latter part of Henry's reign and for the remained of the Tudor period armours of this type, called 'garnitures' today, were used. By the end of the king's reign, the tournament had become a rarity. Jousts to celebrate the coronations of Anne Boleyn and Anne of Cleves were held in 1533 and 1536, but otherwise the king is recorded in a joust

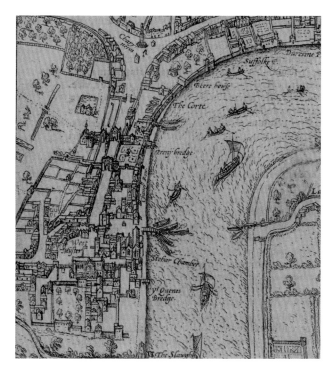

only once, in 1536. A significant exception is the 'May Day Tournament' of 1540, which was a full-scale tournament comprising jousts on 1 May, the tourney on 3 May and the barriers on 5 May, and the king's last great Greenwich garniture, also dated 1540 and designed for all three tournament events, was made for the occasion.

Henry's youthful enthusiasm for the tournament was continued by Edward VI, who staged numerous tournaments throughout his short reign. The young king was not physically able to compete in the joust with his adult court, but showed great skill in running at the ring and other martial sports. Queen Mary continued his enthusiasm for the sport, holding foot tourneys in 1554, four separate jousts, one combined with a tourney, in 1555, and a Shrovetide tourney and Christmas joust in 1556.

Earlier in Elizabeth's reign, jousts to celebrate Shrovetide and Christmas were common, as well as tournaments to celebrate significant weddings within the court, such as those of Henry Knollys and Margaret Cave and of Ambrose Dudley and Anne Russell in 1565, of the Earl of Oxford and Ann Burghley in 1572, and to entertain diplomatic visitors from abroad. Accession Day tilts were held in the tiltyard at Whitehall each 17 November ('Queen's Day'), probably from the year of her accession in 1558 until 1602, the year before her death. First organised by Sir Henry Lee, they became an annual event after 1577, and by 1581 they had become a massive public spectacle. The knights who participated arrived on processional carriages, dressed as heroic or mythological figures with servants costumed to match. A German visitor, Lupold von Wedel, described the scene in 1584:

> Now approached the day, when on November 17 the tournament was to be held, as I mentioned before St Elizabeth's day being November 19. About twelve o'clock the queen and her ladies

▲ Detail of the map of London published by George Braun and Franz Hogenberg in *Civitates Orbis Terrarum*, 1572, showing New Palace Yard and the Whitehall tiltyard.

© The British Library Board, Maps Crace Port I.12

placed themselves at the windows in a long room at Weithol [Whitehall] palace, near Westminster, opposite the barrier where the tournament was to be held. From this room a broad staircase led downwards, and round the barrier stands were arranged by boards above the ground, so that everybody by paying 12d. would get a stand and see the play... Many thousand spectators, men, women and girls, got places, not to speak of those who were within the barrier and paid nothing.

During the whole time of the tournament all those who wished to fight entered the list by pairs, the trumpets being blown at the time and other musical instruments. The combatants had their servants clad in different colours, they, however, did not enter the barrier, but arranged themselves on both sides. Some of the servants were disguised like savages, or like Irishmen, with the hair hanging down to the girdle like women, others had horses equipped like elephants, some carriages were drawn by men, others appeared to move by themselves; altogether the carriages were very odd in appearance. Some gentlemen had their horses with them and mounted in full armour directly from the carriage. There were some who showed very good horsemanship and were also in fine attire. The manner of the combat each had settled before entering the lists. The costs amounted to several thousand pounds each.

When a gentleman with his servants approached the barrier, on horseback or in a carriage, he stopped at the foot of the staircase leading to the queen's room, while one of his servants in pompous attire of a special pattern mounted the steps and addressed the queen in well-composed verses or with a ludicrous speech, making her and her ladies laugh. When the speech was ended he in the name of his lord offered to the queen a costly present, which was accepted and permission given before preparing for the combat. Now always two by two rode against each other, breaking lances across the beam. On this day not only many fine horses were seen, but also beautiful ladies, not only in the royal suite, but likewise in the company of gentlemen of the nobility and the citizens. The fête lasted until five o'clock in the afternoon when Milurtt Lester [Leicester], the Royal master of the Horse, gave the sign to stop. The Queen handed the first prize to the Counts of Ocsenfortt [Oxford] and of Arundel . . .

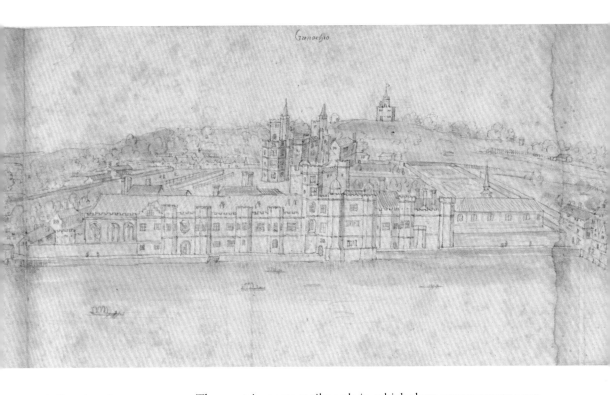

▲ Drawing of Greenwich Palace from the *Panorama of London* by Antonius Van den Wyngaerde, 1558, showing Henry's palace and the tiltyard to the left of it.

© Ashmolean Museum, University of Oxford

The most important tiltyards in which these tournaments were staged were at Westminster, Greenwich, Hampton Court and Whitehall. Henry VIII's early tournaments were all held in New Palace Yard, Westminster, to the side of which Westminster Hall formed a convenient grandstand. The paved area, 120 m long and 63 m wide, was gravelled and sanded, and a tilt barrier erected for the jousts. Following the fire of 1512, the king's tournaments were held at Greenwich, where a tiltyard was situated beside the Palace of Placentia in which the Almain workshop was also housed. The focus then moved to Whitehall, where the tournament to celebrate the coronation of Anne Boleyn was held in 1533. The tiltyard was 147 m long and 24 m wide, and built with a Tiltyard Gallery, 'a sumptuous gallery' where 'the Princes with their Nobility used to stand or sit, and at Windowes to behold all triumphant Iustings, and other military exercises' at its south end, next to the Holbein Gate which connected The Street, outside the Banqueting House, to Whitehall proper to the north. Edward's tournaments were held at Whitehall, Greenwich, Richmond and Blackheath, Queen Mary's at Greenwich, Whitehall, Hampton Court and Hatfield House, but most of Queen Elizabeth's were held at Whitehall. An exception were the jousts of 1575 held at Sir Henry Lee's home at Ditchley.

THE GENTLEMEN PENSIONERS

Henry VIII established a new bodyguard, the Honourable Band of Gentlemen Pensioners, in 1509, a 'new and sumptuous Troop of Gentlemen composed of cadets of noble families and the highest order of gentry'.

Under Henry Earl of Essex they accompanied the king at the battle of the Spurs in 1513 and at the Field of Cloth of Gold in 1520, though they were costly, and the unit was suspended for part of Henry's reign. At Edward VI's coronation they were 'apparelled all in red damask, with their pole-axes in their hands'. The pollaxe, together with a chain and badge, became their distinctive emblems, and versions of these are still carried by their successors. During Elizabeth's reign they were commanded by Henry, 1st Baron Hunsdon from 1558–96, and by his son George from 1596. Renamed the Gentlemen at Arms in 1834, and today, with an establishment of 5 officers and 27 gentlemen, the body survives as the second oldest guard in England, their weapons still in the custody of the Axe Keeper and Butler.

▶ Basket-hilted sword

English, blade German, about 1560. A sword of exactly this type is shown in the portrait of William Palmer. Purchased 1982 from the collection of Claude Blair. IX.2574

◄ Pollaxe

English, early 17th century. The spiked heads of the pollaxes carried by the Gentlemen Pensioners were their characteristic weapon, and versions of the are still carried by their successors, the Gentlemen at Arms, today. This unusual pollaxe may be the only known surviving example from the early period of the unit. Purchased 1986. VII.2044

▲ Portrait, attributed to Gerlach Flicke, of a member of the Palmer family, English, mid-16th century. This oil of panel portrait probably depicts William Palmer, Gentleman Pensioner, about 1539–73, with a pollaxe and basket-hilted sword. Purchased 1998. I.1548

THE ROYAL WORKSHOP AT GREENWICH

The royal armour workshop, or Almain workshop, at Greenwich was founded by Henry VIII. Henry brought to England several groups of foreign armourers, Milanese and Flemings in 1511 and the Almains, from Germany and Flanders, in 1515. The workshop flourished under the Masters Martin van Royne and Erasmus Kirkenar during Henry VIII's reign. From 1567–76 the armoury was under an English Master, John Kelte, and from 1578–1608 the Master was Jacob Halder, a German from Landshut, who moved to London and joined the staff of the Royal Workshop at Greenwich by 1558. He was responsible the finest decorated armour made by the workshop, and recorded in them in his surviving Album of watercolour pictures.

▼ View of the Palace of Placentia at Greenwich. The exact site of the armourers' workshop is still unknown, but it was probably in the complex of buildings just to the west of the palace.

© Bridgeman Images

The workshop at Greenwich was rebuilt between 1515 and 1520, and though its exact location is not known, it is thought to have been just to the west of the Palace of Placentia, on the site of the Greenwich Hospital. In the early 17th century the 'Great Chamber' housed sixteen Greenwich armours and numerous parts of armours,

the 'Workehouse' seventeen armours, mostly unfinished, and most of the tools, 11 stakes, 6 pairs of tongs, 2 vices, 5 forging hammers, 20 small hammers, 2 pairs of shears, 1 chisel, 6 anvils, 2 pairs of bellows, 1 rasp and the 'panne of iron for fire with four wheels' that made up the tool kit of the workshop, while the Cutting House contained 2 forging hammer heads, 2 hand hammer heads, 2 great and 26 small hammers, 4 large and 3 small bicorns, 1 pair of bellows, 5 pairs of tongs, 1 vice, grinding stones and 2 pairs of shears, and the Locksmith's Office contained 1 anvil, 1 stake, 1 bicorn, 2 vices, 4 pairs of tongs, 3 hammers, 1 chisel and 1 pair of bellows.

In lists of 1559 and 1599 the staff was the same, a master, clerk, yeoman, nine hammermen, three millmen, three locksmiths, two labourers, and a part-time gilder.

Continuity and change in the staff of the Royal Workshop at Greenwich

Staff in 1559	Wages per month	Staff in 1599	Wages per month
Erasmus Kyrkenar *Master*	40s	Jacob Halder *Master*	36s
Clerk	36s 10d	*Clerk*	–
James Fuller *Yeoman*	24s	*Yeoman*	–
John Kelte *Hammerman*	38s 10d	John Stephens *Hammerman*	36s
Matthew Diricke *Hammerman*	34s	Thomas Cowper *Hammerman*	36s
Carries Spicarde *Hammerman*	32s	John Garret *Hammerman*	36s
Leonarde Guynell *Hammerman*	32s	Richard Carter *Hammerman*	36s
Hans Mightner *Hammerman*	32s	Richard Hoane *Hammerman*	36s
Jacob Halder *Hammerman*	32s	Thomas Browne *Hammerman*	36s
John Garret *Hammerman*	32s	John Bentley *Hammerman*	36s
Michael Pixe *Hammerman*	32s	William Ratcliffe *Hammerman*	36s
Thomas Cowper *Hammerman*	24s	Richard Stephens *Hammerman*	36s
John Baker *Millman*	22s	Philip Benworth *Millman*	36s
Hans Droste *Millman*	30s	William Chaundler *Millman*	36s
William Barworth *Millman*	30s	John Colgate *Millman*	36s
Richard Stephens *Locksmith*	24s	Clement Robinson *Locksmith*	36s
Henrike Bourman *Locksmith*	24s	William Boreman *Locksmith*	36s
Henry Starkey *Locksmith*	24s	Edward Arnold *Locksmith*	36s
Martin Durris *Labourer*	14s	Richard Messingham *Labourer*	–
John Rugge *Labourer*	15s 4d	Thomas Dolinge *Labourer*	–
Gilder	3s 4d	Daniel Grimes *Gilder*	–

▲ Armourer's stakes

Top: English, 16th century, possibly from the Royal Workshop at Greenwich. A wide variety of stakes were used for hammering out the components of an armour. The stamped mark, WP within a heart, on one of them may be that of William Pickering, Master Armourer at Greenwich 1608–18. XVIII.830 and others from the Tower workshop

▲ Planishing and riveting hammers

English, hafts modern. The armoury contained a large range of hammers of different sorts for different purposes. Presented by F H Cripps-Day, 1942, and others from the Tower workshop. XVIII.97-8

▲ Armourer's shears

English, 16th century, possibly from the Royal Workshop at Greenwich. Four pairs of shears were used at Greenwich, one of them large for cutting out steel plates. Old Tower collection.

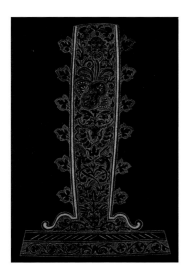

ARMOUR DECORATION: ETCHING AND GILDING IN THE 16TH CENTURY

Etching was first used for the decoration of the steel plates of armour about 1490, probably in the workshop of the Augsburg armour Lorenz Helmschmid. It rapidly became the most popular method of decorating armour and was usually used in conjunction with gilding. Much of the arms and armour made for the Tudor court, especially in the Greenwich workshop, was etched and gilded, often in the Mannerist taste popular at the time. This style, popular throughout Europe in the second half of the 16th century, originated in the rediscovery of the classical world towards the end of the 15th century, and is characterised by the use of figures from Roman history and legend, often framed within panels of strapwork and complex backgrounds of foliage.

First the surfaces of the plate were coated with an acid-repelling substance called a 'resist'. The decorative design was transferred to the coated plate, and the resist then removed to leave the steel surface exposed to the action of the acid. The designs were sometimes drawn specially for the decoration of the armour (Henry VIII's 1540 armour is decorated with designs drawn by his artist Hans Holbein), but more commonly derived from engravings.

The entire ground of the design on the object was then gilded, covered with a thin layer of gold to highlight the detail in the pattern. In the 16th century two processes were used to lay gold onto the surface of the design. The most commonly practiced method was mercury gilding or 'fire gilding'. First the surface of the metal would be cleaned and then wiped with a copper sulphate solution, depositing a thin layer of copper to assist the adhesion of the gold onto the steel surface. An amalgam of gold and mercury was then applied and the plate heated to cause the mercury to evaporate, leaving a thin layer of gold on the surface.

◀ Plates illustrating the process of etching and gilding made by Jack Truscott, formerly the Royal Armouries' gunsmith, in 1999, based on a vambrace from and Italian half armour originally belonging to the Knights of St John of Malta.

THE WAR IN FLANDERS

The Seventeen Provinces (the United Provinces) of the southern Netherlands were established under Spanish rule in the settlement of Charles V in 1549. The widespread adoption of Protestantism in north Europe led to a split from Spain and the Eighty Years War (1568–48), following the signature by most of the Dutch states of the Treaty of Utrecht. Following the Treaty of Nonsuch of 1585, English forces intervened directly against the Spanish in Flanders, but the defeat of the Spanish Armada in 1588 brought this action to an end. The Treaty of Münster of 1648, part of the Peace of Westphalia which ended the Thirty Years war, brought into being the precursor of the modern state of the Netherlands. As the first major challenge to the perception of the divine right of kings, the Dutch Revolt can be seen as the precursor of the English Civil War and the French Revolution.

ROBERT DUDLEY, EARL OF LEICESTER (1533–88)

Elizabeth's favourite, one of her most important courtiers and an active soldier, Dudley served at St Quentin under the Earl of Pembroke in 1557 and was created Knight of the Garter in 1559. A childhood friend of the future queen he was made Master of the Horse to Queen Elizabeth on her accession, and is supposed to have been involved in a long love affair with the queen. His wife, Amy Robsart, died in that year in suspicious circumstances, Dudley was made a Privy Councillor in 1562 and Earl of Leicester with lands at Kenilworth in 1564. In 1578 he secretly married Lettice Knollys, widow of Walter Devereux, 1st Earl of Essex, and was rumoured to have carried on a love affair with her while her husband was alive; some suggested that he was the natural father of her son Robert, 2nd Earl of Essex. He led the campaign to the Netherlands to support

◄ Detail of the etched decoration of Leicester's armour, central medallion is Justice (*Iustitia*), from a series of prints by Etienne Delaune of Paris, about 1560, while in the border above is a battle scene from classical antiquity based on a series of twelve prints by Etienne Delaune, with a contemporary combat with lances at the centre.

◄ Battle scene with soldiers in classical armour, by Etienne Delaune, Paris, about 1561–72. The combat at the right between a cavalry standard-bearer and a foot soldier is at either side of the breastplate's border.
© The Trustees of the British Museum

the Dutch against Philip II 1584–7 during which Sir Philip Sidney died, and returned to England for the Armada preparations in 1588. He had three armours made at Greenwich, only one of which survives.

There were probably three armours designed for Leicester in the Jacob Album but his surviving armour is missing from the Album (there is a gap in the page numbering where it is thought to have been). His first Greenwich armour, a relatively plain small garniture of russet steel with gilt borders, was depicted in a sketch for a portrait by Federico Zuccaro, but the finished painting (now destroyed) showed the Earl in the present armour. It is the first in the Album captioned ER, suggesting the design dates to the earliest years of Elizabeth's reign.

Leicester's surviving Greenwich armour is a small armour 'garniture', with exchange pieces which can be configured for the field and tournament, decorated with recessed bands in the form of ragged staves, all etched and formerly gilt. The decoration, which refers to the bear and ragged staff badge of the Earls of Warwick, includes the Order of the Garter and its chain on the breastplate. The bears depicted on several parts of the armour have collars of the French Order of St Michael, to which Dudley was elected in 1566.

▼ Leicester's first Greenwich armour and its extra pieces from the Jacob Album. Image from *An Almain Armourer's Album*. London 1905.
© Royal Armouries

The armour was made at Greenwich under Jacob Halder. The shaffron, or defence for the horse's head, has its original escutcheon embossed with Dudley's bear and ragged staff badge. This is the only example of embossed work known from Greenwich. The armour is dated stylistically to 1575, and it is thought that it could have been made for the lavish entertainment given by Dudley in Elizabeth's honour at Kenilworth that year.

▶ **Field and tilt armour of Robert Dudley, Earl of Leicester**

Configured for the tilt. English, Greenwich, about 1575. Old Tower collection. II.81

▼ Shaffron of Leicester's armour.

▲ *From top:* Details of the etched decoration of Leicester's armour: the George of the Order of the Garter, the Warwick bear badge encircled by the motto of the Order of the Garter and traces of the original gilding.

▲ Leicester's armour configured for the field.

HENRY HASTINGS, 3RD EARL OF HUNTINGDON (1536–95)

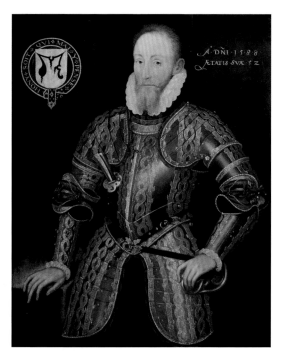

Hastings was knighted at the coronation of Edward VI. He and his father were supporters of Lady Jane Grey, and to seal the political alliance Hastings married Katherine Dudley, the future Earl of Leicester's sister, in 1553. Father and son were imprisoned in the Tower by Queen Mary. Hastings was restored under Queen Elizabeth and appointed one of the joint custodians of Mary Queen of Scots during her imprisonment. As a reward for this service he was created a Knight of the Garter in 1570. In 1572 he was appointed president of the Council of the North, replacing the ineffective 3rd Earl of Sussex in that office, and subsequently became Lord Lieutenant, a post he occupied until his death. A devoted Protestant, he secured the execution of no less than 30 Catholic clergy in York.

▲ Portrait of Henry Hastings, 3rd Earl of Huntingdon, English, dated 1588, wearing his brother-in-law Robert Dudley's second Greenwich armour, now lost. I.46

◄ Leicester's second Greenwich armour and its extra pieces from the Jacob Album. Image from *An Almain Armourer's Album.* London 1905.

© Royal Armouries

SIR PHILIP SIDNEY (1554–86)

Elizabethan poet, courtier and soldier, Sir Philip Sidney was the eldest son of Sir Henry Sidney and Mary, sister of Guilford Dudley, husband of Lady Jane Grey, and of Robert Dudley, Earl of Leicester. From 1575, following a cultural tour of Europe, he joined Queen Elizabeth's court, and in 1577 was sent on an important mission to convey the queen's condolences to the Holy Roman Emperor Rudolf II in Prague on the death of the previous emperor Maximilian II. He returned to England and to court, but found time to start his great epic romantic poem, *Arcadia*, and to publish his collection of sonnets and songs, *Astrophil and Stella*. He was patron to many authors, including the poet Edmund Spenser, the travel writer Richard Hakluyt and the scholar Justus Lipsius. He attempted to leave

▲ Portrait of Sir Philip Sidney probably by Cornelius Ketel, 1578.
© National Portrait Gallery, London

◄ Embossed shield

Probably of Sir Philip Sidney, embossed with a central medallion depicting Hercules shooting the centaur Nessus, after an engraving by Marcus Gheeraerts, Flemish, mid- to late 16th century.
AL.160 1

On loan to the Royal Armouries from the Verschoyle-Campbell family

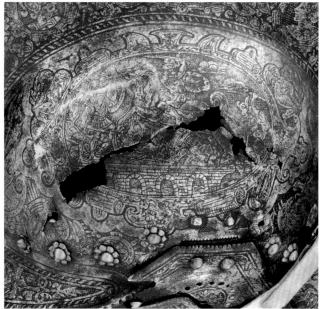

Burgonet of Sir Philip Sidney

With etched and gilded
decoration by Adrian Collaert,
Flemish, Antwerp, about 1583.
The main features of the
decoration show scenes of
Roman legend, including on
the left side Horatius Cocles
holding the Sublician Bridge
over the Tiber against the
Etruscans. Bequest of
Dr R. Williams, 1974. IV.569

with Sir Francis Drake for the West Indies in 1585, but was summoned back to court and appointed governor of Flushing. This office he resigned to Peregrine Bertie 'my very special friend'. He fought the Spanish in the Low Countries under the command of the Earl of Leicester, and was fatally wounded at Zutphen by a musket shot. His funeral at St Paul's Cathedral in London was a huge affair with 700 mourners, and was recorded in a panoramic engraving by Theodore de Bry. His home, Penshurst Place in Kent, still preserves his funerary helm and its porcupine crest.

Sidney's surviving armour was made in the Low Countries, probably in Antwerp, and decorated there by the engraver Adrian Collaert. The armour elements, a burgonet, gorget, breastplate, backplate and shield, are all decorated in the Mannerist style so popular in north Europe in the late 16th century. The sources used for the decoration are mostly engravings by the Parisian artist Etienne Delaune, but include prints by Marcus Gheeraerts the Elder, Virgil Solis and Giulio Romano. The gorget shown here is dated 1583, and another helmet, a 'Spanish' morion in the Metropolitan Museum of Art, New York, is signed by the decorator. Though dispersed in the 19th century, all the pieces can be traced back to Penshurst.

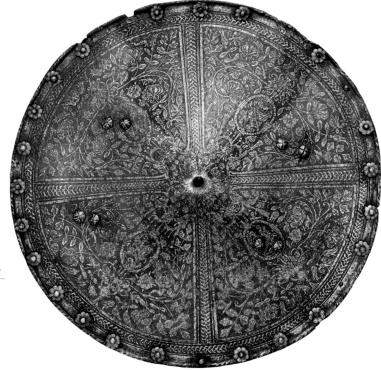

▶ Shield of Sir Philip Sidney

With etched and gilded decoration by Adrian Collaert, Flemish, Antwerp, about 1583. AL.160 2

On loan to the Royal Armouries from the Verschoyle-Campbell family

▲ Gorget of Sir Philip Sidney

With etched and gilded decoration by
Adrian Collaert, Flemish, Antwerp,
dated 1583. Purchased from the collection
of Sir James Mann, 1983. III.1692

◄ Breastplate of Sir Philip Sidney

With etched and gilded decoration by
Adrian Collaert including a battle scene
in the central cartouche, Flemish,
Antwerp, about 1583. III.1218

▼ Backplate of Sir Philip Sidney

With etched and gilded decoration by
Adrian Collaert, including a central
figure of Mars, based on an engraving
by Etienne Delaune of Paris, Flemish,
Antwerp, about 1583. III.1220

Detail of the breastplate.

PEREGRINE BERTIE, 13TH BARON WILLOUGHBY D'ERESBY (1555–1601)

◀ Portrait of Lord Willoughby d'Eresby, probably an 18th-century copy of a late 16th-century original. I.67

▼ *Below right:* Page from the Jacob Album showing the set of extra pieces from which the armet is the only surviving piece.
© Victoria and Albert Museum, London

▼ Armet

From the Greenwich armour of Peregrine Bertie, Lord Willoughby d'Eresby. English, Greenwich, about 1580. Bequeathed by Dr Richard Williams, 1974. From the Hengrave Hall collection. IV.577

Grandson of Henry VIII's brother-in-law Charles Brandon, Duke of Suffolk, Bertie was sent to the household of Sir William Cecil as a boy, later married Mary de Vere, daughter of the Earl of Oxford, and inherited the barony in 1581. He was sent on diplomatic missions from 1582, with Leicester to the Netherlands and alone to invest Frederick II of Denmark with the Order of the Garter. He fought with Leicester and Sidney in the Netherlands in 1586–8 and was the hero of Zutphen, in which he led a celebrated cavalry charge. He subsequently served as a general 1588–90. After the death in office of Henry Carey, 1st Baron Hunsdon, he was appointed as Governor of Berwick.

This armet skull is all that remains of a decorated Greenwich armour. The extra pieces for this armour with its distinctive broad etched and gilt bands of guilloche are illustrated in the Jacob Album, but the main page (on which the owner was usually named), is missing. However, Lord Willoughby is illustrated wearing the armour in this and other versions of the portrait, and it is generally thought most probable that the armour was his.

THE ARMADA CAMPAIGN

A great Spanish invasion fleet under the Duke of Medina Sidonia sailed against England in 1588. The plan was to rendezvous with the Spanish army under the Duke of Parma off the coast of Flanders, then land in England. The fleet was pursued along the English Channel by an English fleet under Lord Howard of Effingham, Sir Francis Drake and Sir John Hawkins, attacked by fire ships and defeated by superior gunnery at Gravelines. It was forced around the coast of Scotland, and many of its ships were wrecked on the coast of Ireland as they tried to return to Spain.

◀ Field armour of Sir John Smythe. II.84

ALESSANDRO FARNESE, DUKE OF PARMA (1545–92)

Nephew of Philip II of Spain and Don John of Austria, the Duke of Parma was a Spanish soldier who fought with Don John at Lepanto against the Turks in 1571 and in the decisive battle of Gembloux against the rebel Dutch in 1578. After the death of his uncle he was appointed governor of the Netherlands, commanded the Spanish armies in Flanders against the Dutch 1584–87 and commanded the invasion army that the Spanish Armada was to have transported to England in 1588.

◀ Portrait of Alessandro Farnese, Duke of Parma, in armour. Italian, late 16th century. I.980

SIR JOHN SMYTHE (1534–1607)

Smythe was first cousin to Edward VI through the sister of his mother, Jane Seymour. He fought as a volunteer in France and the Low Countries from the early 1550s, and during the 1560s in Hungary and in the Mediterranean against the Turks. He returned to England in 1572 and was granted the manor of Little Baddow in Essex. In 1576 he was knighted and appointed ambassador to Spain, undertaking a mission there in the following year. In 1587 Smythe was commissioned to train troops against the threat of the Spanish invasion in 1587, but, snubbed and discredited by the Earl of Leicester, he retired to a life as a military writer. He is best known for his book, *Certain discourses: concerning the formes and effects of divers sorts of weapons, and other verie important matters militarie, greatlie mistaken by divers of our men of warre in these daies; and chiefly of the mosquet, the caliver and the long-bow; as also, of the great sufficiencie, excellencie, and wonderful effects of archers*, published in 1590, in which he argued (unsuccessfully) for the reintroduction of the longbow into the English army. In 1596 he engaged in a drunken tirade against military service overseas, for which he was imprisoned for sedition in the Tower until 1598, after which he retired into obscurity.

▲ Illustration of the armour in the Jacob Album. Image from *An Almain Armourer's Album*. London 1905.
© Royal Armouries

Smythe's Greenwich armour is a field garniture comprising a three-quarter-length light cavalry armour worn with mail sleeves, with a half-shaffron and saddle steels, alternative long tassets, and a 'Spanish' morion for wear on foot. It is decorated with broad recessed bands etched and gilt with strapwork decoration on a blackened ground, with classical figures and the motto FUTURA PRAETERITIS ('the future from the past', from one of Pliny's *Letters 7.27*). As well as a shield, the armour originally had a pair of gilt stirrups and a pair of pistols associated with it. The burgonet and buffe appear to have been made in Augsburg and decorated en-suite with the rest of the armour in Greenwich. The circular shield or *rondache* for infantry use

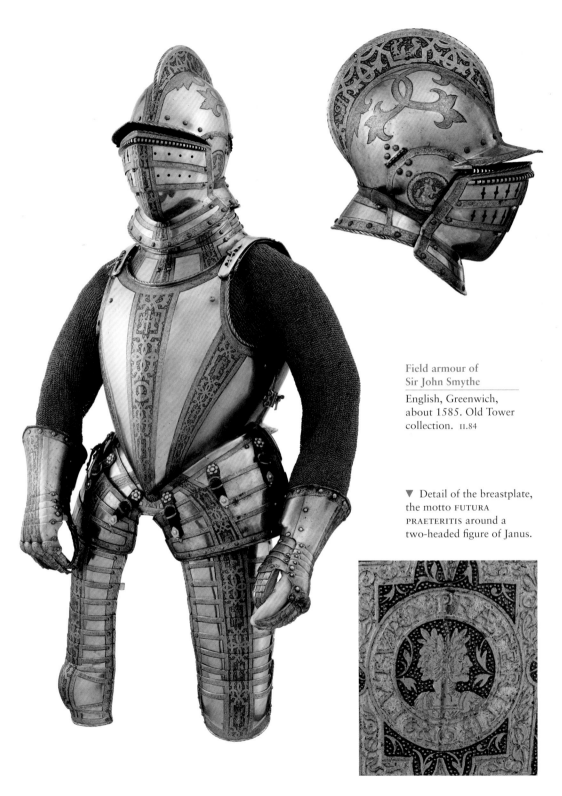

**Field armour of
Sir John Smythe**

English, Greenwich,
about 1585. Old Tower
collection. II.84

▼ Detail of the breastplate,
the motto FUTURA
PRAETERITIS around a
two-headed figure of Janus.

is in the Metropolitan Museum of Art, New York, and was certainly made in Augsburg as it is stamped with the town's mark on the inside. Another gauntlet for the armour is on loan to the Royal Armouries from the Maidstone Museum (originally from West Wickham Church, Kent), and two similarly decorated gauntlets are in St Steven's Church, Canterbury, associated with the monument of Sir Roger Manwood. The armour appears in the Jacob Album immediately after Pembroke and Hatton, but the page showing its extra pieces is missing. However the composition of the extra pieces is very similar to the first armour of Sir Henry Lee, which, like the Smythe armour, was also substantially made 'beyond see'. On the backplate, for example, the legendary Roman Mucius Scaevola, widely used in art as a symbol of courage and duty appears on the left, Etienne Delaune's Justice at the right.

▲ Long tassets, and a 'Spanish' morion for wear on foot.

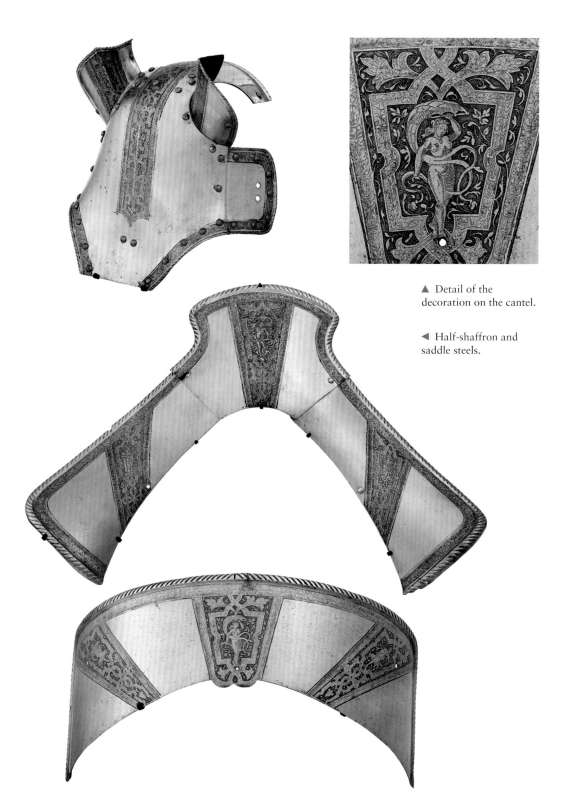

▲ Detail of the decoration on the cantel.

◀ Half-shaffron and saddle steels.

SIR WALTER RALEIGH (1552–1618)

Born in Devon to a family closely associated with the court, Raleigh was registered at Oriel College Oxford and the Middle Temple, but seems to have spent little time in either. He fought with the Huguenots against the French Catholics at Jarnac in 1569, and for the English in suppressing the Desmond Rebellion in Ireland, becoming an Irish landlord, and a favourite of Queen Elizabeth. He organised two expeditions to found the colony of Roanoke in America, in 1584 and 1588, but the colony failed. He joined Essex in the raid on Cadiz in 1596. On the death of Elizabeth and accession of James I Raleigh was implicated in the 'Main plot' to overthrow the new king. He was imprisoned in the Tower 1603–16, and after a last voyage seeking El Dorado he was tried and executed for treason. He was an accomplished poet, regarded as one of the best of the Elizabethan age, and although he did not introduce the potato or tobacco to England, was probably responsible for making the latter fashionable at court. None of his personal armour or arms are known to survive.

◀ Engraved portrait of Sir Walter Raleigh. British, mid-19th century. I.132

SIR FRANCIS DRAKE (1540–96)

Born near Tavistock in Devon, Drake learned his seamanship and the techniques of piracy from members of the Hawkins family based in Plymouth. In 1562–3 John Hawkins made vast profits from capturing slaves from Portuguese ships and transporting them on to the West Indies. In the 1571–5 and 1577–80 he organised his own expeditions to the Americas, plundering Spanish possessions and trade, the second voyage continuing across the Pacific into a complete circumnavigation. In 1584 he was funded by Leicester, John and William Hawkins and Sir Walter Raleigh, as well as the Queen herself, in an expedition against the Spanish West Indies. In 1587 Drake led the successful attack on Cadiz, and was one of the senior commanders of the fleet which defeated the Spanish Armada in 1588. This was followed by a failed expedition in 1589 against Portugal, and another against the Canaries in 1595–6 in which Drake fell ill and died. Drake is remembered for his innovations in ship-board gunnery and his mastery of the naval assault of ports, as well as finishing his game of bowls at Plymouth before sailing against the Armada.

▶ Engraved portrait of Sir Francis Drake. British, mid-19th century. I.128

GEORGE CLIFFORD, 3RD EARL OF CUMBERLAND (1558–1605)

Born at Brougham Castle, Cumbria, Clifford succeeded as earl in 1570 and became a ward of the crown. Looked after by the Earl of Bedford, he was educated at Cambridge, and became a favourite at Elizabeth's court. Nicknamed her 'rogue', he was appointed Queen's Champion in 1590 as successor to Sir Henry Lee, and made a Knight of the Garter in 1592. He served in the Armada campaign on board a royal ship, and in 1589–98 undertook privateering voyages on royal ships against the Spanish off the Azores and in the West Indies, capturing numerous treasure ships and the port of San Juan, Puerto Rica, in 1598. After the succession of James I in 1603 Clifford was appointed to the new king's Privy Council, and served as Warden of the West and Middle Marches on the Scottish borders. His surviving Greenwich armour, which includes in its etched and gilded ornament of combined Es for the Queen, is one of the most finely decorated of the series, and the preparatory watercolour for it in the Jacob Album the most skilfully executed.

Clifford's decorated Greenwich armour, a tournament garniture decorated with broad etched and gilded bands on a russet ground, was preserved in Appleby Castle, and is now in the Metropolitan Museum of Art, New York (no. 32.130.6). The watercolour of the armour and its extra pieces in the Jacob Album is of finer quality than all the others, and was presumably not executed by Jacob Halder. Unusually some of the exchange pieces were not coloured in, and appear not to have been made.

 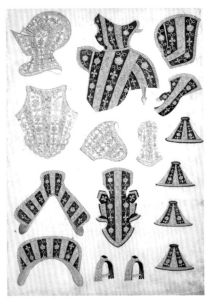

◀ Illustration of the armour in the Jacob Album.

© Victoria and Albert Museum, London

HORACE VERE, BARON VERE OF TILBURY (1565–1635)

Francis Vere was fighting in the Low Countries in the war against Spain by 1585, was joined by his younger brother Robert in 1589 and by their youngest brother Horace in 1590. In 1596 he was appointed lieutenant colonel in Sir John Wingfield's regiment and took part in the Earl of Essex's expedition to Cadiz. On the death of its colonel, he took command of the regiment and was knighted by Essex. Later that year he entered service in the Dutch army and played a major part in the battle of Nieuwpoort in 1600 in which his brother and Prince Maurice of Nassau defeated the Spanish under Albrecht of Austria. Robert was appointed Master General of the Ordnance in 1616.

▶ Portrait of Horace, Lord Vere of Tilbury. Oil on panel, attributed to George Gower, dated 1594. I.104

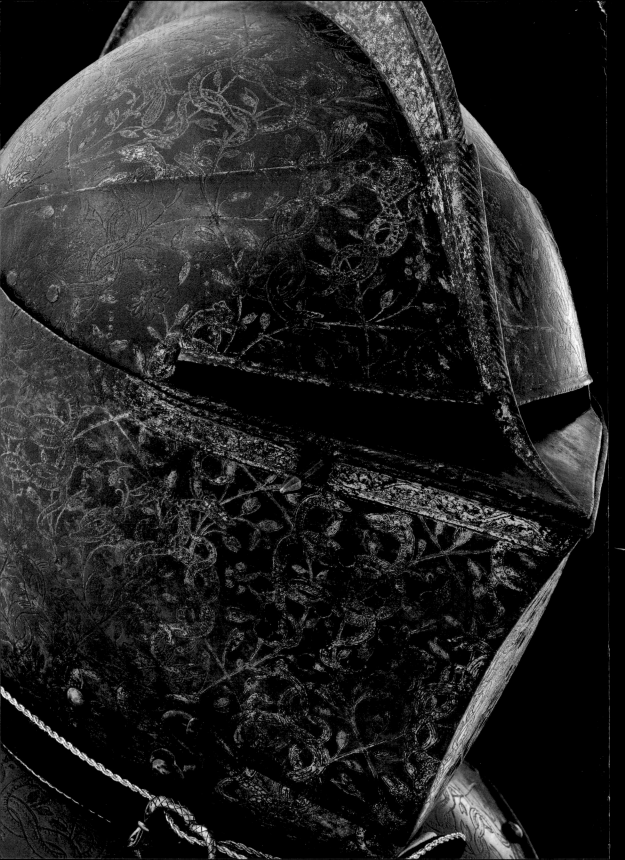

EQUIPMENT FOR THE ARMY AND NAVY

The Elizabethan army had three branches, the cavalry, infantry and artillery. A few cavalry were still equipped as lancers, with complete armour from head to toe, and a lance and sword for combat use. More of the cavalry were equipped as demi-lances, with three-quarter armour, a sword and a light lance or, increasingly, a pair of pistols.

◄ Side view of the close helmet from a three-quarter field armour of Henry Wriothesley, 3rd Earl of Southampton. II.360

▼ Woodcut from Derricke's *History of Ireland*, published in 1581, showing an English force with demi-lances in three quarter armour, infantry harquebusiers in 'Spanish' morions and pikemen in corslets.

During Elizabeth's reign the proportion of cavalry equipped with firearms was on the increase, and the majority of these were armoured only with a cuirass with mail sleeves and an open-faced burgonet on their heads. The requirement for all-round vision and dexterity to manage the loading of the firearms outweighed the requirement for heavy armour. By 1575 the national musters showed only 270 demi-lances but 2,700 light cavalry. This was a tactical change, not forced by any lack of equipment. In the 'Armorie of the Tower of London, a Reporte of the Complete Armor there' of 1588, there were still 1,300 complete lance armours in store there, and 1,138 demi-lances.

▲ Side view of the
close helmet from the
same armour.

◄ Demi-lance armour

Probably Flemish,
about 1560, from the
Pembroke armoury at
Wilton. II.164, III.1269

The crucial technological advance which had made this development on the 16th-century cavalry possible was the production of reliable firearms which could be used easily on horseback. The wheellock had a mechanism in which the sparks to ignite the priming powder in the pan next to the touch-hole were provided by a serrated wheel rotating rapidly against a piece of iron pyrites. Once 'spanned' or wound up with a key, the weapon could be discharged simply by squeezing the trigger. The snaphance, a type of mechanism particularly favoured in England, achieved ignition by striking a flint, held in the jaws of a cock, against a steel striking surface on the end of an arm positioned over the priming pan. These weapons represented the most advanced military technology of the day.

A typical company of English infantry in 1584 comprised 80 pikemen and 40 billmen as its heavy infantry contingent, while 80 harquebusiers or calivers and 40 archers formed the 'shot'. The pike, the primary mêlée weapon of the infantry, was composed of a slender steel point attached to a 5.4 m (18 ft) long ash shaft, and was wielded in two hands. The bill, the characteristic English medieval hafted weapons, which had its origins in an agricultural implement, continued to be used in England by the shock troops who were equipped on the continent with the halberd. Another survival from the Middle Ages was the longbow; despite the reorganisation of the English army late in the reign of Henry VIII, the old medieval weapons still had a substantial role in the Elizabethan army. The firearms used by the infantry were the caliver or harquebus and the recently introduced musket, a longer weapon supported by a forked rest and firing a heavier lead ball. Both of these weapons were fired by the simple matchlock mechanism, in which a length of smouldering match-cord, held in the jaws of the swivelling serpentine,

▼ Military figure by Jacob de Gheyn after Henrik Goltzius, 1587. I.128

was lowered into the priming powder by squeezing the trigger. While simple, this mechanism was awkward and required live fire and two hands to use, which made it unsuitable for use on horseback.

The heavy infantry, armed with pikes or bills, were equipped with half armours called corslets. These were made of the same components as the cavalry demi-lance armours, but with shorter tassets covering the thighs, allowing greater leg movement, and with open-faced helmets called morions. In 1561 there were in the armoury at the Tower 7,719 'Flanders corsletts' imported from the Low Counties and 7,597 'Almayne corsletts' imported from the German armour centres, especially Nuremberg. These had almost completely replaced the old-fashioned Almain rivet, the infantry half armours introduced by Henry VIII, of which only 900 'lacking diverse parcells' remained in the armoury. The 'Reporte' of 1588 records 2,390 'Flaunders corslettes' and 2,990 'Almayne corsletts' showing the large numbers that had been issued in preparation for the Armada threat.

As Elizabeth's reign progressed there was a tendency to lighten the harness of the infantry in the field. Cosbie, a captain in Willoughby d'Eresby's company of 1589 to France, not only complained of the equipment of his troops and supplied them with Spanish morions of his own, but instructed his men to throw away their 'poldrons, vambraces and tasses as being incumbrances without use' to the horror of their commander who had provided them at his own expense.

Interior of the same morion, showing the lining band to which the original lining was sewn.

▶ 'Spanish' morion

Probably Flemish, about 1580. Tower armoury. IV.451

The same officer found fault with the equipment of the men. While inspecting them he found that some had 'white' (bright steel) burgonets and others black, while others had the old-fashioned comb morion with its high crest, 'now most unpopular'. The corslets too were not of the new, fine shape. It was pointed out to him that the mixed collection of helmets supplied would serve just as well on the battlefield, even if they did not make such a brave show on the march, and that the old, flat-bellied breastplates would withstand the push of pike just as well as the new ones.

The shot, however, were protected only by the morion and occasionally by the characteristic English defence of the period, the jack of plates. This, often called a coat of plates, was a quilted doublet inside which small square iron plates were sewn, and which were occasionally provided with sleeves also protected with plates. These jacks were particularly popular for sea service. In 1561 they were recorded as 'on the ships, 2,000' together with 2,000 'skulls' 550 corslets and 1,330 'murrions'.

▲ 'Spanish' morion

Flemish or English, about 1580. IV.2018

► Comb morion

Probably Flemish, about 1580. IV.449

Back view

◀ Jack of plate
English, about 1560.
Tower armoury. II.27

Back view

▲ Jack of plate with
plate sleeves

English, about 1580.
Purchased 1985. III.1884–5

Soldier, politician and favourite of Queen Elizabeth, Devereux was probably named after his godfather Robert Dudley (according to popular gossip, his natural father), who became his stepfather after his mother Lettice remarried. He succeeded as earl in 1576, while still a minor, and was taken in hand by William Cecil, Lord Burghley, the Lord Treasurer. After graduating at Cambridge in 1578 he stayed first with the Dudleys at Kenilworth Castle, then with the Earl of Huntingdon at York. By 1587 he was a favourite of the queen, and was created a Knight of the Garter in 1588. In the same year he succeeded Dudley as Master of the Horse on the death of his stepfather. Despite his lack of military experience he succeeded in

▲ Portrait of Robert Devereux, 2nd Earl of Essex, after Marcus Gheeraerts the Younger, about 1597. I.43

◄ Burgonet

English, Greenwich, about 1580. IV.529

snubbing experienced soldiers such as Sir John Smythe. His experiences of leading English armies was unsuccessful. He led an expedition to Normandy in 1591, and most disastrously to Ireland in 1599. In 1600, on his unauthorised return to London he attempted to force an audience with the queen with the support of several nobles, an act for which he was tried and executed for treason. One black field armour for Essex remained in the workshop at Greenwich in the early 17th century, and the portrait of Essex I by William Segar in the National Gallery of Ireland shows him in a plain black armour, perhaps the one he wore 'all in Sable sad' at the Accession day tournament of 1590.

Because the armour illustrated on this page is plain it has never been possible to identify its original owner. The Royal Workshop made many armours in the late 16th and early 17th centuries, for infantry ('footman's armor) and cavalry ('fielde armor complete' or 'tilte armor compleate'), both black and white (left black from the hammer or polished bright respectively), and it is unknown whether all were decorated or some left plain. One was a 'white Tilte armor compleate for the Kinges Maiesty' for James I, and it is tempting to identify this armour with the king. The portrait of Essex by William Segar in the National Gallery of Ireland shows the earl in a black version of a very similar armour, however. The armour was used in the Line of Kings display at the Tower from 1660 as the armour of William the Conqueror, and is still affectionately known by that name.

▶ Plain field and tilt armour.

English, Greenwich, about 1590.
Old Tower Collection. II.40

HENRY WRIOTHESLEY, 3RD EARL OF SOUTHAMPTON (1573–1624)

Henry Wriothesley, 3rd Earl of Southampton, was a great scholar and lover of the arts, and is best known as the only acknowledged patron of William Shakespeare. For his financial support, the poems *Venus and Adonis* and the *Rape of Lucrece* were dedicated to him. Southampton was also a military and political figure like his grandfather, Thomas Wriothesley, 1st Earl of Southampton, who had been Lord Chancellor under Henry VIII. In the 1590s Southampton campaigned at Cadiz, the Azores, Ireland and in the Low Countries. He incurred the wrath of Queen Elizabeth by secretly marrying one of her ladies in waiting, Elizabeth Vernon, in 1598. In 1601 he participated in an insurrection with Essex against the queen and was sentenced to death. Luckily for him, his sentence was commuted through the intervention of his patron, Sir Robert Cecil, to life imprisonment in the Tower of London, where he was accompanied by his cat, Trixie, who appears with him in one of his portraits. Elizabeth's death and the accession of King James I led to his pardon in 1603 and his creation as a Knight of the Garter in the same year. Southampton also has a significant American connection; he funded an expedition to New England in 1602, was a signatory of the second charter of the London Company of Virginia, and served as its treasurer in the 1620s. He died in 1624, commanding a regiment of volunteers fighting the continued struggle for Dutch independence from Spain.

▼ Detail of the etched and gilded decoration of Southampton's three-quarter field armour.

Southampton's armour, identified from the portrait, a three quarter or demi-lance armour for use on the battlefield, it may have been obtained when the earl was sent to Paris in 1598 as part of a diplomatic mission. Its fire-blued surface is beautifully acid-etched and gilded with an overall design of entwined snakes and vines, rendered in the Mannerist style popular in late 16th-century northern Europe.

**Three-quarter field armour
of Henry Wriothesley,
3rd Earl of Southampton**

French or Flemish, about 1600.
Purchased 1984, following a
by public appeal, donors to
which included the National
Art Collections Fund,
the National Heritage
Memorial Fund and
Sir Emmanuel Kaye, from the
collection of Lord Astor of
Hever Castle, Kent, having
been acquired by him from a
London dealer in 1907. II.360

◀ *Page 80*: Portrait of
Southampton, English
School. On loan to the
National Gallery from the
Portland Estate.

© National Portrait Gallery, London

SWORDS AND DAGGERS OF THE TUDOR COURT

The character of the swords carried by the nobility changed completely during the Tudor period. During Henry VIII's reign the basket-hilted broadsword evolved from the old, cross-guarded medieval sword. During Elizabeth's reign a completely new type of sword became popular, the rapier. This weapon with its complex guard and long, slender blade, was accompanied by a whole new style of swordsmanship, introduced by the new fencing masters of Italy and France, in which intricate play with the point replaced the cut and thrust of the broadsword. The new rapiers were often accompanied by matching daggers, and fencing with sword and dagger was a new skill expounded in the fencing manuals which became essential for the education of gentlemen. These new swords, like the armour and clothes with which they were worn, were often highly decorated, and became a status symbol for the wealthy as well as practical arms.

▲ Military figure by Jacob de Gheyn after Henrik Goltzius, 1587. I.128

►▼ Rapier

Probably English, late 16th century. Complex guards like this are known as 'swept hilts'.
The environment of the river Thames is excellent for the preservation of edged weapons. This example is completely preserved by the river, with its original grip covered in brass wire basketwork. A similar excavated hilt has the date 1594, and a very similar sword is shown in a portrait of John Shirley dated 1588. Purchased 1977. From the river Thames at Queenhithe, 1976. IX.1494

◄▼ Basket-hilted broadsword

Probably English, about 1540. Purchased 1993, from the river Thames at Southwark Bridge. IX.4427

▶ Quillon dagger

Right: Probably English, late 16th century, matching exactly the Queenhithe rapier. It also retains its original hilt with wooden grip bound with steel wire. Its blade is etched with floral ornament and the Latin motto NON VI SED SAPIENTIA (not with force but wisdom) 159?. Another almost identical example also from the Thames is dated 1597. Purchased 1978, from the river Thames at Bull Wharf, 1978. X.589

▶▼ Rapier

North Italian, about 1600. The hilt is lavishly decorated in gold counterfeit damascening with strapwork and foliage. The contrast between the gilding and the blued steel is characteristic of the Mannerist taste of the period. The wire-bound grip is modern. Purchased 1947 from the Ledger collection, formerly in the Brett and Visconti collections. IX.869

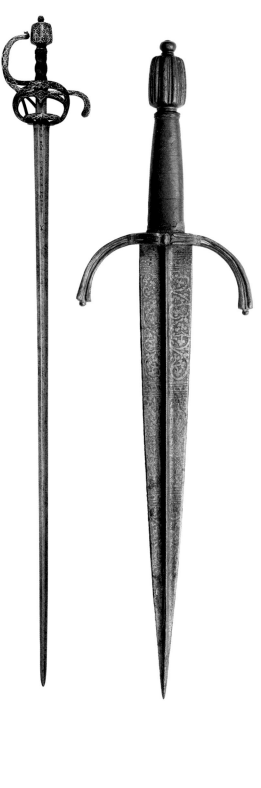

Riding sword

English, about 1600, reputedly presented to a member of the Weatherby family by Queen Elizabeth I. This is one of the finest English swords of its period. It has an iron hilt decorated with arabesque patterns in gold damascening, and with cinquefoil flowers, wild strawberries and ears of corn encrusted in silver, within borders of raised and filed rope-work. The grip,

which is covered in fish skin bound with silver wire, is later. The blade is stamped with an unidentified maker's mark in the form of a double cross near the hilt. Similar hilts are depicted in portraits of Sir Henry Wriothesley, 3rd Earl of Southampton (1573–1624) and of Henry Prince of Wales (1594–1612) by Robert Peake the Elder in the National Portrait Gallery. Purchased 1983, from the collections of Lord Astor at Hever Castle. IX.2594

FIREARMS OF THE TUDOR COURT

As new types of firearms were developed for military purposes they were simultaneously adopted by the nobility for hunting and sport. Like the armour they wore and the swords they carried, their firearms were lavishly decorated, as a testimony to their wealth and taste. Very few firearms from the Elizabethan court survive, but the selection illustrated here gives a sense of the lavish ornamentation of their weapons.

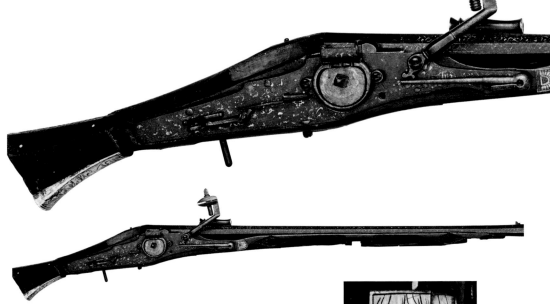

Wheellock pistol

Probably Flemish, about 1550. This poorly preserved gun was originally superbly decorated. The decoration which remains on the barrel is characteristic of the Spanish sword maker and damascener Diego de Caias and his pupil Damianus de Nerve, who worked in London for Henry VIII from 1543 until the king's death in 1547. Most of the bone plaques with which the stock was originally covered are lost, but one, decorated with the figure of a man in Tudor costume, remains.
Presented by the Metropolitan Police, 1992. XII.10250

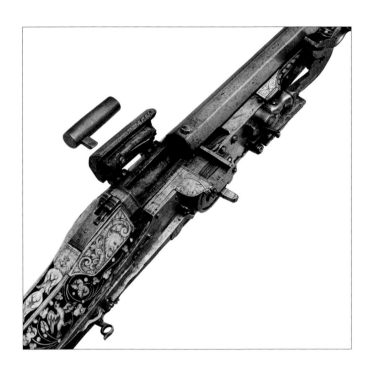

Breech-loading wheellock gun

German, about 1575. Attempts to make effective breech-loading guns began early in the history of firearms. This 32-bore gun has a hinged breech section into which ready loaded iron cartridges were fitted. The barrel and lock are relatively plain, with sea monsters on the wheel-cover, but the stock is inlaid with stag horn panels finely engraved with owls and other birds, monsters and hunting scenes, the figure of Lucretia, the legendary Roman noblewoman who stabbed herself after being raped by the Etruscan Tarquinius Superbus, probably after the engraving of Lucas van Leiden of 1514, and an unidentified armorial. Purchased 1998. XII.11127

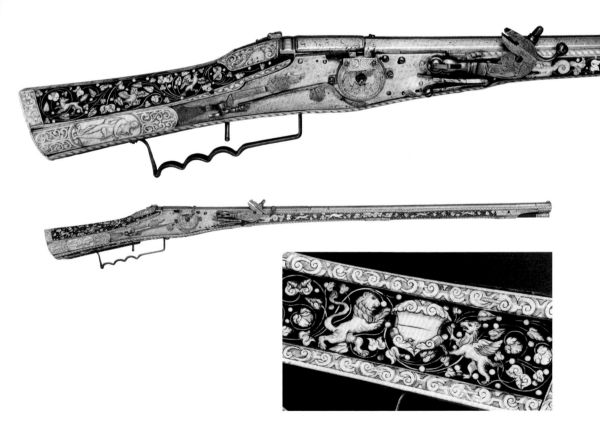

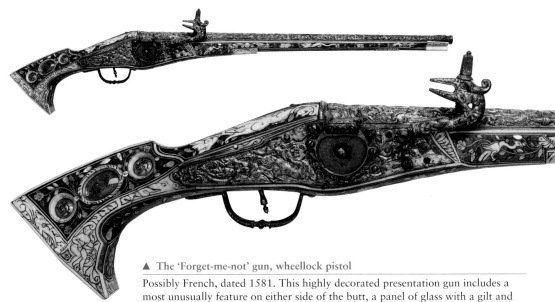

▲ The 'Forget-me-not' gun, wheellock pistol

Possibly French, dated 1581. This highly decorated presentation gun includes a most unusually feature on either side of the butt, a panel of glass with a gilt and painted backing (*verre églomisé*) with a sprig of forget-me-not flowers and the inscriptions *ver gis mein nit* (forget me not) and the ihs (the start of the name of Jesus in Greek) monogram within a sacred heart. The lock and barrel are chiselled and gilt with satyrs and sphinxes, and the stock is inlaid with bone decorated with profuse ornament in the Mannerist style popular in north-west Europe in the late 16th century. Purchased with the aid of the National Art Collections Fund, 1960. By tradition owned by an English family since the 16th century. XII.1764

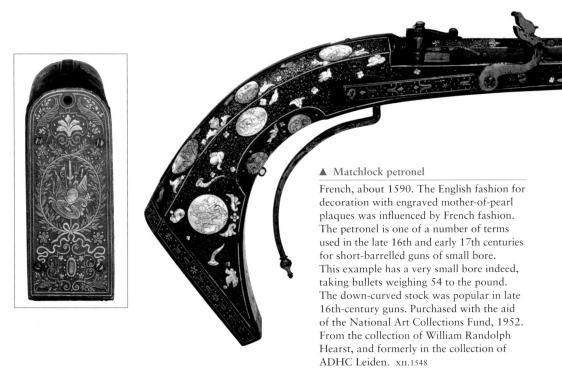

▲ Matchlock petronel

French, about 1590. The English fashion for decoration with engraved mother-of-pearl plaques was influenced by French fashion. The petronel is one of a number of terms used in the late 16th and early 17th centuries for short-barrelled guns of small bore. This example has a very small bore indeed, taking bullets weighing 54 to the pound. The down-curved stock was popular in late 16th-century guns. Purchased with the aid of the National Art Collections Fund, 1952. From the collection of William Randolph Hearst, and formerly in the collection of ADHC Leiden. XII.1548

▲ Wheellock sporting rifle

Probably Saxon, about 1590. This short barrelled
hunting rifle is decorated in a characteristic German
style, the wooden stock completely covered with
panels of stag horn engraved with Mannerist
ornament, birds, dogs and stags on a dense ground
of floral scrolls in strapwork panels. The butt plate is
decorated with arms of Saxony, and the goddess
Venus features on the butt trap. Presented by the
National Art Collections Fund, 1942, from the
collection of Beriah Botfield at Norton Hall. XII.1197

▼ Snaphance pistol

English, about 1600. The stock of this pistol is of
walnut decorated in the characteristic English style
of the later years of Elizabeth's reign with panels of
horn and mother-of-pearl. Pistols of this quality are
associated with royal gifts; a pair of similar pistols in
the Kremlin Armoury, Moscow, formed part of a gift
from King James I to the Russian Tsar Boris
Godunov in 1604. Purchased 1971 with the aid of
the National Art Collections Fund. XII.1823

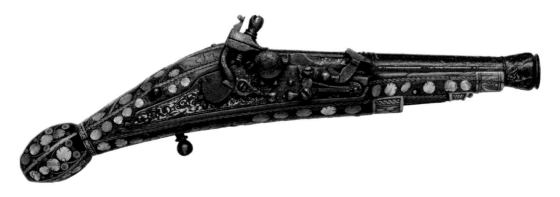

PARTS OF A GREENWICH TOURNAMENT GARNITURE

Two pages from the Jacob Album showing Sir Henry Lee's second armour with its extra pieces. Image from *An Almain Armourer's Album*. London 1905.

© Royal Armouries

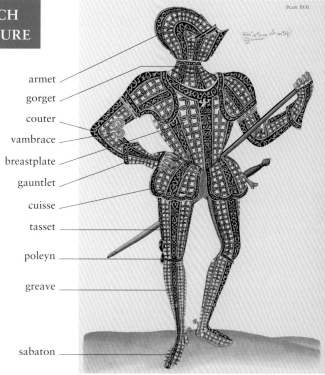

PLATE XVII.

armet
gorget
couter
vambrace
breastplate
gauntlet
cuisse
tasset
poleyn
greave
sabaton

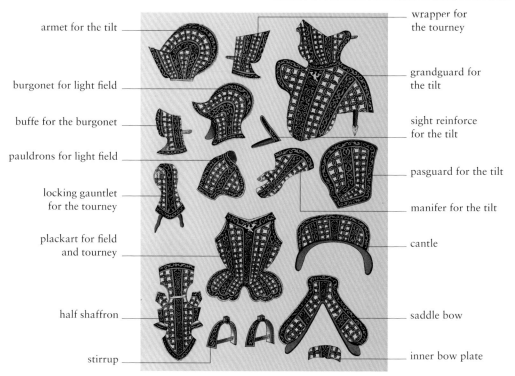

armet for the tilt

wrapper for the tourney

burgonet for light field

grandguard for the tilt

buffe for the burgonet

sight reinforce for the tilt

pauldrons for light field

pasguard for the tilt

locking gauntlet for the tourney

manifer for the tilt

plackart for field and tourney

cantle

half shaffron

saddle bow

stirrup

inner bow plate

GLOSSARY

anime — Cuirass is made with articulated plates, popular in the mid-16th century, probably intended to look like the ancient Roman armour we now call the *lorica segmentata*.

armet — Helmet enclosing the whole head, opening with large cheekpieces at either side which fasten at the chin. The term is used indiscriminately with close helmet in contemporary documents, but modern usage is to separate the two types.

arming doublet — Quilted jacket designed for wear under armour, often fitted with mail sleeves and with 'points' for the attachment of armour pieces.

backplate — Solid plate defence for the rear of the chest, comprises the cuirass with the breastplate.

bevor — Face defence worn with an open faced helmet, such as the sallet in the 15th and early 16th centuries and incorporated into the close helmet in the 16th and early 17th centuries as the chin defence. In close helmets, often made in two, the upper and lower bevor, both articulated on the same pivots as the visor, sometimes called the lower visor.

bill — Infantry weapon popular in 15th- and 16th-century England based on the agricultural hedging tool.

bore — Measurement of the internal diameter of a firearm, often expressed as fractions of a pound weight (so 12 bore=1 1/3 oz or 37.8 g) Small bore refers to larger bore values, large bore to smaller values.

breastplate — Solid plate defence for the front of the chest, comprises the cuirass with the backplate.

breath — Ventilation holes or slots in the upper bevor of a close helmet other form of helmet fully enclosing the head.

broadsword — Broad, straight-bladed sword, usually with a single edge, often with a sharp 'false edge' at the point.

brow reinforce — Additional plate often forming part of the visor protecting the upper front of a helmet such as a sallet, close helmet or armet.

buffe — Face defence worn with the burgonet in the mid- to late 16th century, often articulated in order to fold down (see 'falling buffe').

burgonet — Open-faced helmet with a peak and cheekpieces popular in the 16th and early 17th centuries. Often styled after the helmets of classical antiquity.

butt plate — Solid plate at the rear of the butt of a firearm.

butt — Rear section of the stock of a firearm, held against the chest or rested against the shoulder in the case of long-arms, gripped by the hand in the case of pistols.

barrel — Tubular section of a firearm in which the charge and bullet are placed when loaded.

cabasset — Open-faced helmet with a flat brim and a 'pear stalk' at the apex of the skull; this French term is sometimes used for what are called 'Spanish' morions in 16th-century England.

caliver — Or harquebus, short-barrelled, usually small-bore gun held in two hands for discharge, fired from the chest or shoulder.

cantle — Rear section of a saddle, also 'cantle plate', the steel reinforce for the rear of a saddle.

cheekpieces — Plates attached to the skull of a helmet to protect the cheeks, fastening the helmet closed by joining at the front on an armet, secured under the chin on a burgonet or morion.

close helmet — Helmet enclosing the whole head, opening with a visor and one or two bevors pivoted an the same pivots at either side of the skull. The term is used indiscriminately with armet, but modern usage is to separate the two types.

collar	Throat defence, formed of front and rear main plates and usually three narrow lames above for the neck, articulated to allow movement. Also 'gorget.
comb morion	Open faced helmet with a brim usually swept upwards at the front and rear, the skull expanded into a broad comb or crest along the centre line.
corslet	Half armour for infantry service in the mid- to late 16th century
couter	Plate defence for the elbow, forms the vambraces along with the upper and lower cannons of the vambraces.
cuirass	Defence for the chest formed of back and breastplate.
cuisse	Defence of plate for the lower thigh, articulated to the poleyn and strapped to the leg.
demi-lance	Cavalryman in three-quarter armour, armed with a sword and light lance. Also used of an armour for such a cavalryman.
embossing	Mechanical process in which a design is beaten into metal which has been placed on a pliable anvil of pitch, sand-filled cushion or wood resulting in raised and/or sunken areas.
engraving	Mechanical process in which a chisel or pointed tool such as a burin is used to create an incised design. Technically difficult and usually confined to small areas.
etching	Chemical process in which a corrosive solution such as sulphuric acid is used to remove metallic material not protected by an applied resist of wax or oil paint. A highly popular decorative technique used on both arms and armour.
extra pieces	Additional components for an armour, decorated en suite with it, enabling it to be configured for different tournament events and battlefield roles. Also 'pieces of exchange' or 'exchange pieces'.
falling buffe	Face defence worn with the burgonet in the mid- to late 16th century, articulated in order to fold down (see 'buffe').

fauld	Articulated lames below a breastplate forming a short skirt, to which the tassets are attached.
garniture	Modern term for an armour provided with extra pieces enabling it to be configured for different tournament events and battlefield roles.
gauntlet	Plate defence for the hand, composed of a solid tubular cuff, articulated metacarpal lames covering the rear of the hand, either formed as a fingered gauntlet, with finger and thumb defences of iron scales riveted to leathers, or as a mitten gauntlet with articulated plates covering the fingers.
gorget	Throat defence, formed of front and rear main plates and usually three narrow lames above for the neck, articulated to allow movement. Also 'collar'.
grandguard	Reinforcing plate for the tilt, shaped to cover the left shoulder and left front of the helmet. Evolved in the early 16th century from the shield.
great bacinet	Form of helmet popular on the battlefield in the early 15th century, survived into the early 16th century for use in the foot combat. Formed of a deep skull extending over the shoulders, a matching deep plate bevor and a large visor for the face; in the early 15th century only the visor was pivoted, but by the late 15th century both bevor and visor were articulated by the same pivots at either side of the skull.
great helm	Form of helmet popular on the battlefield in the 13th and 14th centuries, survived into the early 16th century for use in the tilt. By the late 15th century, very similar to and often called a great bacinet. Formed of a deep skull extending over the shoulders, a matching deep plate bevor combined with a visor for the face, swept forward at the sight which are usually stepped, pivoted at either side of the skull.
greave	Plate defence for the lower leg, often made in one with the 'sabaton', usually joined by turning pins and studs to the 'poleyn'.

half shaffron	Plate defence for the upper part of a horse's head. Often spelt 'chanfron' and other similar spellings.
harquebus	Or caliver, short-barrelled, usually small-bore gun held in two hands for discharge, fired from the chest or shoulder.
halberd	Hafted infantry weapon comprising a cleaver-like axe blade, rear spike and from the late 15th century a broad stiff top spike. From the German 'Halm' a staff and 'Barte' an axe.
inner bow plate	Steel plate for the inner part of the saddle bow, provided as part of a garniture at Greenwich.
jack of plates	Quilted doublet inside which small square iron plates were sewn, occasionally provided with sleeves also protected with plates. Popular for sea service in mid- to late 16th-century England.
joust	Single combat on horses using lances.
lance	Cavalry spear or the cavalry armed with such spears, equipped with full armour.
lock	The ignition mechanism of a firearm, see 'matchlock,' 'wheellock' and 'snaphance'.
locking gauntlet	Plate mitten gauntlet for the right hand used in the tourney in the mid-16th century, designed with extended finger plates allowing them to be fastened to the cuff at the inside of the wrist, securing a sword in the hand so it cannot be dropped.
longbow	Bow usually made of yew wood, about 6 ft (1.8 m) in length, used especially by English archers of the 14th–16th centuries.
mail sleeves	Arm defences made of mail, often sewn to an arming doublet, worn under plate vambraces to protect the gaps or as independent defences.
manifer	Reinforce for the left hand for the tilt, worn over the vambraces and gauntlet, and with the 'pasguard' and grandguard' to provide additional protection in the tilt for the left side of the body.
matchlock	Ignition system for firearms using smouldering match cord held in a pivoted serpentine, lowered by activated the trigger into the priming powder in the pan of a gun.

morion	Open faced helmet with a brim usually swept upwards at the front and rear, and termed a 'Spanish morion or a 'comb morion, or with a flat brim and sometimes called a 'cabasset', though these were also called 'Spanish' morions in 16th-century England.
musket	Long-barrelled, usually large-bore gun held in two hands for discharge, fired from the chest or shoulder with weight of the barrel usually supported by a rest or musket rest.
pasguard	Reinforce for the elbow for the tilt, worn over the vambraces and fastened to the couter, with the 'manifer and grandguard' to provide additional protection in the tilt for the left side of the body.
pauldron	Plate defence for the shoulder, usually formed of a main plate with articulating plates above and below, usually manufactured with a cut-out for the lance at the armpit of the right pauldrons.
petronel	Small harquebus, short-barrelled, small-bore gun either held in two hands for discharge, fired from the chest or shoulder, or held in one hand as a large pistol.
pike	Long spear used by infantry in the 14th–17th centuries, held in two hands, often 3.5 m. in length. Pikes were introduced into the English army in the 1540s.
pistol	Short-barrelled, small-bore gun held in one hand for discharge.
plackart	Reinforcing breastplate attached to the breastplate by pierced studs and turning pins, worn for tourney or heavy battlefield use.
points	Laces made of heavy, waxed thread used for the attachment of armour pieces.
poleyn	Plate defence for the knee, usually made with a heart-shaped wing at the outside to protect the tendons of the knee joint, articulated by lames to the 'cuisse', and attached to the greave by studs and turning pins.
pollaxe	Long-hafted axe used on the battlefield by men-at-arms in the 14th and 15th centuries, and used

	in the foot combat and by some bodyguards in the 16th century and later. Derived from 'poll', a head rather than 'pole', a length of wood.
priming powder	Fine gunpowder placed in to pan of a firearm, connected by the touchhole to the main charge of gunpowder inside the barrel.
rapier	Form of sword with a long, slender blade intended exclusively for thrusting, popular in the 16th and 17th centuries
riding sword	Light, relatively short-bladed sword intended for civilian use.
rondache	Circular shield, used by some infantrymen, usually of all-steel construction, also called a buckler, targe or target.
sabaton	Plate defence for the foot, formed of articulated lames riveted at either side and with internal leathers at the centre, of ten combined with articulated defences for the ankle and permanently joined to greaves.
saddle bow	Font section of a saddle, also 'bow plate', the steel reinforce for the front of a saddle.
saddle steels	Set of plates for the front and rear of a saddle, see 'saddle bow' and 'cantle'
shaffron	Plate defence for the head of a horse.
sight	Vision slit in the visor of a close helmet armet or other form of helmet fully enclosing the head.
sight reinforce	Additional plate provided in a very few 'garnitures' to give additional protection to the sight of an armet or other helmet fully enclosing the head, for use in the tourney.
snaphance	Ignition system for firearms using a flint held in the jaws of a spring-loaded cock and released by the trigger to strike sparks from a pivoted steel or frizzen to ignite the priming powder in the pan of a gun.
'Spanish' morion	Open-faced helmet with a flat or swept brim and a 'pear stalk' at the apex of the skull; sometimes the French term cabasset is used for helmets of this type with a flat brim.
stock	Wooden part of a firearm providing a bed for the barrel and lock,

	including the butt which enables the gun to be conveniently held for firing.
swept hilt	Complex form of guard for a rapier popular in the late 16th and early 17th centuries.
tasset	Plate defence for the upper thigh, usually attached by straps and buckles or by hasps to the 'fauld' of the 'breastplate'.
toe-caps	Plate defences for the toes. Foot defences formed of mail shoes with plate toe-caps were popular in the mid-16th century.
tourney	Or tournament, or hastilude. Strictly a mass combat of knights but embraces a wide range of martial displays.
vambrace	Plate defence for the arm, comprising upper and lower cannons and 'couter' at the elbow. The term rerebrace for the upper cannon of the vambrace and vambrace for the lower cannon were in common usage in the 14th century, but by the 16th the word vambrace was used for the whole defence.
vamplate	Circular plate attached in front of the grip of a lance for the tilt, providing extra protection for the right hand.
visor	Plate defence for the face in many forms of helmet, especially the 'armet' and 'close helmet'. The terms upper and lower visor are sometimes used for the visor and upper bevor of a close helmet.
wheel-cover	Part of the lock mechanism of a wheellock, plate fitting over the rotating wheel to protect it, often decorated.
wheellock	Ignition system for firearms using a spring-loaded grooved wheel which when released by the trigger spins against a piece of iron pyrites held in a pivoted dog to strike sparks to ignite the priming powder in the pan of a gun.
wrapper	Plate reinforce for a helmet fully enclosing the head, particularly the armet, which has a vulnerable point where the cheekpieces join at the front of the chin. Used in the tourney in the 16th century, also on the battlefield in the 15th century

FURTHER READING

Blair, C 1958 *European armour*. London

Blair, C 1962 *European and American arms c. 1100–1850*. London

Blair, C 1985 Greenwich armour. *Transactions of the Greenwich and Lewisham Antiquarian Society* 10: 6–11

Blakeley, E 1997 The tournament garniture of Robert Dudley, Earl of Leicester. *Royal Armouries Yearbook* 2: 55-63

Borg, A 1976 Two studies in the history of the Tower Armouries. 1: Heads and horses from the Line of Kings. *Archaeologia* 105: 317–32

Cripps-Day, F H 1934, *Fragmenta Armamentaria. 1, An introduction to the study of Greenwich armour*. London

Cruikshank, CG 1968 *Elizabeth's army*, Oxford

Dillon, H A 1905 *An Almain armourer's album: selections from an original MS in the Victoria and Albert Museum, South Kensington*. London

Doran, S (ed.) 2003 *Elizabeth: the exhibition at the National Maritime Museum*, London

Eaves, I 1999 The Greenwich armour and locking-gauntlet of Sir Henry Lee in the collection of the Worshipful Company of Armourers and Brasiers. *Journal of the Arms and Armour Society*, 16 September: 133–64

Edge, D 1992 The Greenwich field armour of Thomas Sackville. *Park Lane Arms Fair 9*, London: 5–11

Norman, A V B 1980 *The rapier and the small sword 1460–1820*. London

Pyhrr, S W and J-A Godoy 1998 *Heroic armour of the Italian Renaissance: Filippo Negroli and his contemporaries*, New York

Richardson, T 2009 The Royal Armour Workshops at Greenwich, in G Rimer, T Richardson and J P D Cooper, *Henry VIII, arms and the man 1509–2009*, Leeds: 148–154

Rimer, G 2001 *Wheellock firearms of the Royal Armouries*, Leeds

Williams, A and A de Reuck 1995 *The Royal Armoury at Greenwich, 1515–1649: a history of its technology*, London

Young, A 1987 *Tudor and Jacobean Tournaments*, London

The right of Thom Richardson to be identified as the author of this work has been asserted in accordance with the Copyright Designs and Patents Act 1988.

Series Editor: Debbie Wurr
Series Designer: Geraldine Mead
Series Photographers: Gary Ombler, Rod Joyce

Acknowledgements: Thanks to Gary Ombler for new photography, to Chris Streek for organising the images, Jack Truscott for the section on etching and gilding, and to all my colleagues for help with the work that enabled this publication over the years, especially Graeme Rimer, Ian Eaves, Paula Turner, Alison Watson and Keith Dowen.

Royal Armouries Museum, Armouries Drive, Leeds LS10 1LT

ISBN 978-0-948092-73-2

Printed by W&G Baird